Take, eat, for this is the body of the blues. And drink the spirit of these sublime—the sublime as opposed to the merely beautiful has terror in it—and hardwon pain-songs sung in communion with and compassion and advocacy for all the haunted and wounded, the innocent defiled ones who now have their voices. Norbert Krapf's *Catholic Boy Blues* is a poetry of trauma and trembling faith.

William Heyen, author of *Shoah Train* and *A Poetics of Hiroshima*

Catholic Boy Blues is a significant book not just because of its subject matter. It will be a great comfort to men and women who were abused, to the families of such victims, but also to the great body of Catholics who have faith in the church and its priests and are ashamed of the failure of the church leadership to confront the abusers, to level with the victims and their families, and to admit their complicity in the cover up. It is ironic that something called the Blues can rejuvenate the human spirit.

John Groppe, *Emeritus Prof. of English, St. Joseph's College, IN*

These searing, savage, heartbroken, fearlessly naked poems take us into the depths of the agony that early sexual abuse causes and explore the fiery alchemy that leads from brutalized silence to molten outrage to forgiveness. This is a major work which deserves the widest readership throughout the Catholic Church and far beyond.

Andrew Harvey, author of *The Hope: A Guide to Sacred Activism.*

Catholic Boy Blues

A Poet's Journal of Healing

For Sonia,
w/ thanks for your poems,
your friendship,
& your support
of these bluesy
poems!

Norb
South Bend
July 12, 2014

Catholic Boy Blues
A Poet's Journal of Healing

Norbert Krapf

Photograph taken by the author's pastor and given to his parents in the 1950s

Greystone Publishing LLC
Nashville, TN
www.greystonepublishing.com

Catholic Boy Blues
by Norbert Krapf

FIRST EDITION, 2014

Hardcover - ISBN 978-1-941365-01-4
Softcover - ISBN 978-1-941365-00-7
E-Book   - ISBN 978-1-941365-02-1
Copyright 2014 by Norbert Krapf

Cover Images:
Front cover photograph taken by the author's pastor and
given to his parents in the 1950s.

Back cover photograph © 2012 Richard Fields.

Book Design: Megan Curtin Greystone Publishing LLC

Greystone Publishing LLC
Nashville, TN

www.greystonepublishing.com

For my sisters and brothers

of any age

in all lands

abused by priests

or other authority figures

I been in the blues all my life. I'm still delivering
'cause I got a long memory.

Muddy Waters

Through me many long dumb voices...

Walt Whitman, "Song of Myself"

Who hears may be incredulous.
Who witnesses, believes.

Emily Dickinson

Contents

I. Counting the Collection

II. The Boy and the Man He Became

III. Tell Me, Pastor

IV. The Priest on Sorry

Preface

For fifty years, I did not want to write these poems.

Not because I wanted to avoid the subject of childhood abuse, but because I did not want to make a reputation as a poet who in childhood was sexually abused by his parish priest. I never denied the abuse in my past, had in fact told Katherine, who became my wife in 1970, about it before we married, but only in general terms. I wanted to put that part of my past behind. I would not allow it to "ruin" my life, the life I would make despite it. I would have my marriage, family, and career, as educator and writer. Move on, not look back. I would transcend this darkness.

Things changed, however, when both of us retired from teaching in the New York area for thirty-four years and moved back to Indiana in 2004. Before then, whenever I read about the sexual abuse scandals around the country, I would become outraged. In every case, the details I read about matched the situations I remembered. Always there were skeptics who doubted the veracity of survivors' testimony, but I knew better. I had been there. My nose recognized the stink of an ugly Catholic truth.

When I read about a priest in Indianapolis who was accused of abusing boys in three parishes here and was transferred to Spencer County, in my native southern Indiana, where he continued his pattern of abuse, I was even more outraged. Too close to home. My silence came close to reaching its limits. I had to do something, testify, even though a part of me still did not want, nor was ready, to go public.

When a friend, my wife, and I went on retreat together in December 2006, I decided to book my first session of spiritual direction with the director of the center, whom our friend recommended highly. Would I tell this woman about the childhood abuse now consuming my thoughts? I would decide upon meeting her. When I entered the room and saw her sitting, calmly, in the corner with a silent smile, I knew I must speak. What this gentle but firm spiritual director, a nun, said after I made my declaration changed my life. "Norbert," she replied quietly, "how can you write about this?"

I was shocked at first, because I did not want to honor the topic by acknowledging its significance in writing. I knew immediately that if I wrote poems on this dark subject, I would be obliged, by my responsibility and mission as a poet, to share them with the public, to help others. By then I had made a reputation writing about my southern Indiana origins, including my growing up in a German Catholic community, in a series of poetry collections and later, in the forthcoming prose memoir, *The Ripest Moments: A Southern Indiana Childhood.* This memoir I began in early 1998, not long after my mother died, set aside for almost seven years until we moved to Indianapolis, and finished in the fall of 2004 and early 2005. The writing of this memoir brought me closer to the secret I still kept.

Soon after the retreat, the poems in *Catholic Boy Blues* began to come, with volcanic force, night and day. I was astonished by the almost total recall of details from fifty years earlier. There were a hundred poems in what became the first section, the most I thought the topic deserved. After a short respite, another hundred came, which I thought would surely be the end. Then came fifty more and I was again sure I was done. At that point, a skilled and compassionate therapist asked a question that disarmed me. Would I consider writing poems in the voice of The Priest? I did not want to, did not think I could or should. Up to that point, the poems were in the voices of the boy, the man I became, and a choric, grandfatherly, and folksy Mr. Blues, who arose out of my love for the rural blues that developed during the late 60s when I was a graduate student at the University of Notre Dame.

How could I speak for my abuser? Why would I want

to? No choice, really. I did not realize, for a day or two, that the rhythms of the voice and the way of thinking of my priest abuser were still registered in my psyche, available for recall. The poems started erupting again, until I had a total of 325, which I set aside for three years, to give myself distance from them, continue to heal, and prepare myself for going public. The time had come to testify, to help other victim-survivors, many of whom, like me, preferred to keep their stories to themselves. I wanted to reach and help them. As I say in one of the poems, "One voice singing by itself can / sound awfully small, but several / voices lifting as one can make / a chorus that sings a mighty song." As I learned, it is healthy to sing, the blues in particular.

In winnowing through the 325 poems in December of 2010 and, after another respite, again in September of 2011, then editing and revising once more in December and early January, 2012, I decided to break with previous practice in structuring collections and, as much as is artistically viable, place the poems in the order in which they were written. Why? To represent the rocky road toward forgiveness and healing as it actually takes place within a particular abuse victim-survivor. This journey is not a straightforward linear progression from A to Z. I quickly discovered that after an expression of anger over some recalled episode and apparent equilibrium, another memory can arise that arouses further anger, resentment, hurt, sorrow. This return to a previous complex of emotions, or new variations on it, is evident in the blues and plays an important role in the process of recovery. I have tried to honor this pattern in so far as it does not impede the reader's movement through the book. I wanted not to censure, or diminish by rearranging the sequence of, the voices that arose from within me.

Two poems (as well as a few others) whose genesis is described in the Acknowledgements came later, "Angel

of Power and Protection" (August 2010) and "Words of
a Good Priest" (June 2013). Their vision of looking back
toward darkness and forward into light made them good
candidates to serve as prolog and epilog for this book that
came of sixty years of living with this story of childhood
abuse, trying to put it in perspective, and working to move
beyond it so that the writing and telling of this story might
help the author and others heal. *Catholic Boy Blues* appears
a few months after I turned seventy.

Despite the pain of returning to this aspect of my
childhood, I am grateful for the experience of meeting
the boy I was, the man I became, my friend and mentor
Mr. Blues, and even The Priest, whom I have tried to give
his convoluted, self-serving say. I have sometimes been
astonished by their monologues, dialogues, and colloquies
and would be glad if they could speak in a play one day
in which Mr. Blues, and maybe the others, sing or half
sing, half talk their lines. I hereby thank them all for (re)-
introducing themselves to me. Each of them has contributed
to my arc of moving from the depths of darkness toward the
coming of light. May they speak to you, dear reader, as you
begin your excursion into this book. May you too have faith
in the power of poetry to heal. As the greatest American
poet once said, I stand somewhere waiting for you.

—Norbert Krapf

Introduction by Matthew Fox

The poet Derek Walcott, in accepting the Nobel Prize for poetry in 1992, declared that "the fate of poetry is to fall in love with the world in spite of history." This powerful statement reminds us of the darkness that so much history contains—the wars, the injustices, the mistakes, the crimes, the malfeasance, the lies. History tempts us to give up on life. Poetry and other art forms are gifts from the gods that allow us to endure, to heal and to thrive in spite of history.

Lately, first in the Roman Catholic Church, and in the football hierarchy of Penn State University, one shadow side of history, the rape and abuse of children and the cover up by powers that be, has been making headlines and telling us things about ourselves and our institutions that we prefer not to hear. Denial reigns. Adultism rules when institutional ego and reputation take precedence over the safety of children whether that institution is a university or a church. In this book, from an acclaimed poet laureate, we hear the truth that burns through denial and we pray once again that the truth will make us free.

After armies of lawyers and (somewhat) contrite bishops and football coaches and in-denial popes there cometh the poet. A poet-victim to tell the truth, sing the truth, speak the truth, gather the truth with facts and heart and the only weapons victims have ever possessed—the truth-telling that alone leads to redemption, prevention, healing and ultimately compassion and forgiveness.

These poems tell what a steep price the soul pays for childhood abuse. How many years (over fifty in the present poet's life) of keeping the secret; how much damage was done in his and other families, he keeps asking. What a price a community pays as well. A close-knit German Catholic community no less. Former Pope Benedict XVI would do well to take a retreat immediately with these poems in hand and read and pray these poems and then tell the world why his all-powerful office of the Holy Inquisition, responsible for wayward clergy, did not end child abuse by priests, some of whom, such as the infamous Father Maciel, were so highly favored by his boss, Pope John Paul II, who is getting canonized. And, while he is at it, let Cardinal Ratzinger (retired Pope Benedict XVI) tell the world why his office kept the lights on late at night to beat upon holy and hard-working theologians but kept mum on perverse pedophile priests.

Hopefully the new Pope Francis will take the suffering of the children more seriously than did his two predecessors and instigate reforms that hold clergy and the hierarchy responsible for abuse and its elaborate cover ups.

In these poems the poet speaks the truth not just about the *facts* but also about the feelings. The stories. The broken lives. The betrayals. The many others also abused. The hypocrisy. The religious hypocrisy. The spiritual hypocrisy. The losses. The anger. The sadness. The grief. The distance traveled from religion, from church, from oneself.

The probing here of the depth of passion and loss (what the mystics call the "Via Negativa") is profound. And universal. All grief speaks this way. All grief is angry and wild, sad and sorry, mute and silent, even secret. But not forever. Breakthrough is so needed. Breakout is so important. This book is a breakout book. The truth must be spoken (not just adjudicated, not just financially reimbursed through fines in civil court). This is why Walt Whitman can say "The true Son of God comes singing his song." The Jesus story reminds all men and women that the truer we be sons and daughters of God, the surer we will be crucified.

Innocent boys, like the innocent Christ, wanted only to love life and explore it fully and, with an overly naïve

and trusting parish community and sister and parents, were
befuddled by the adult lies, the religious lies going on.
They are, sadly, still going on. The church is not reforming
or even trying to reform itself. Quite the opposite, it has slid
(and even rushed) backward into a defensive mode again of
superiority "beyond which there is no salvation," a mode
of authoritarianism that condemns the whistle blower, the
prophet, the thinker as trouble-maker. The church is what it
is, unfortunately.

But the poems live. They are organic and truthful.
They speak the truth more loudly than sermons and rituals
and papal bulls; more appropriately than fancy colored
vestments and rote readings from holy books. They reach
to the soul, to the heart, to the Spirit. They bear the mark
of authentic preaching of salvation and of a living Christ of
compassion.

They are the door and the holy gate that open wide to
light and Spirit. The author learned, of necessity, how to
live and love and heal and work outside the dead walls
of a decaying church and the wounded parameters of his
broken soul. It is amazing that he has led the fruitful life
he has as a college professor, as a poet, as a husband and a
father of two adopted children. William Jay Smith, former
U.S. Poet Laureate, commented on Norbert Krapf's poetry
for a blurb used on the back cover of his prose memoir,
The Ripest Moments: A Southern Indiana Childhood, this
way: "Not since Theodore Roethke has any poet handled
so successfully the subject of youth and adolescence." How
is it possible that a person can tell his childhood story so
successfully in prose and poetry while leaving out the
truths that are alive in the present book? What does this say
about the strength of the man? What does it say about the
strength of our species, that we can keep on keeping on?
This collection of poems fills out the memoir of a loving
but wounded childhood. It is what Meister Eckhart called

"a denial of denial." That is what breakthrough is all about.

The poet tells us the secrets he has learned about life not only in this book but in his many other volumes, such as the retrospective *Bloodroot: Indiana Poems* and *Sweet Sister Moon,* that sing numinously of the wonders of the land, its creatures, its trees and seasons, its animals and soil. Listen to his praise of the Indiana woods: "My father loved to go hunting in the woods. Later I understood that what he loved most about hunting was the serenity and the calm palpable in the earliest hours of the morning when, with the slightest hint of light dawning behind the outline of trees, the natural world begins to awaken and sing. Or in the evening when a hush settles over the forest, darkness begins to descend, and the silence expands....every time I went on one of those holiday hunts with the Schroeder clan, I had the feeling that time was suspended and we were all part of something that went way beyond us, beyond our time, and maybe even beyond our place....I begged and prayed for time to stand still and the day to never end" (209, 228). Or this poem, "The Figure in the Landscape," to the goddess in nature:

I found my goddess
in the lay of the land
I love, in the curves
of her rolling hills,
the rise and spread
of trees in her woods,

in the tangle of weeds and wildflowers
that grow lush
in her fallow fields,
in the way she opens herself to rain
and accepts the snow
and swells and heaves
in the hot sun.

Without such praise (what the mystics call the "Via Positiva"), I believe, the prophet's soul would not have survived long enough to sing these blues, these lamentations. The Via Positiva holds the Via Negativa as Rilke taught us when he said: "Walk your walk of lament on a path of praise." The praise, let us be clear, is decidedly *not* a praise of the church institution or its ruling class so busy covering up and denying its own sins and hypocrisy. It is not a praise of history. The praise is for *creation* and the heart and mind behind it. The praise is for the Creator.

The poet's many songs of praise reveal how resilient the human soul is. For forty years Norbert Krapf has been recognized as a praise poet, one who championed the beauty and blessing of his native Indiana soil and landscape and habitat and eco-magic and small towns. It will be startling to many what he reveals in these poems, that in the midst of so much beauty there was also moral carnage going on—in the name of religion no less—and that it took him fifty years just to come to grips with it all. Amidst all the light of growing up in the green mid-west, there was also massive shadow. But see it he does. And in doing so he carries out the deep vocation of the artist: To tell the truth, the beautiful truths and the painful truths.

We learn in this collection, and from a statement in the Preface, how rich a healing aid the poet received when he discovered the blues while a graduate student in the late 1960s at Notre Dame. Thus Mr. Blues, whom the victim-survivor discovers within himself while confronting his pain, plays a significant role in this book, entering periodically like a Greek chorus or like the sage elder that he is, counseling balance and patience with the healing process. This collection is a tribute to the power of music and the blues in particular to help us stay true to the truths that the Via Negativa and the Dark Night want to teach us.

The thirteenth century Beguine mystic Mechthild of

Magdeburg reminded us that in life we drink two kinds of wine—the white wine of joy and the red wine of suffering—and that "until we have drunk deeply of both we have not lived." White wine has dominated the author's previous poetry, but not exclusively. In *Blue-Eyed Grass: Poems of Germany,* he has written of the darkness of World War II and the Holocaust and confronts the realities of the red wine that is part of his German heritage. He has also written about a racial incident from his college years in "Fire and Ice," a poem that received the Lucille Medwick Memorial Award from the Poetry Society of America, and a cycle about the Miami Indians, including the slaughter of innocent women, children, and elders referred to in history books as "The Battle of the Mississinewa."

The life of the man and his work of poetry unveils for all who read it an observer not only of the pain of life but of the wonder and beauty and gratuity of it all. One almost wonders if the pain the poet suffered as a child was not a sort of initiation into a shamanistic vocation such as Walt Whitman or David Palladin underwent that allowed them to live in two worlds at once, the visible and the curtained world, as well as the two worlds of the Via Positiva and the Via Negativa. Is it possible that the poet's pain, so thrust into his memory against his will as a youth, was also a kind of wild fire that sent him off to college, heavy drinking during those same summers while working in his hometown, so near the scene of the abuse, and on to the New York area, out of nature's bosom and beyond into heavy searching for the good, searching for a reason to live and to love and to work and to parent and to sing of blessing?

In making this deep journey the poet comes around to being a healing shaman. For these poems are not his but all of ours. Now we can all make the journey with the anawim, the dispossessed, those without a voice, the abused, whether or not we have been there ourselves. And, as Meister Eckhart tells us, "a healing life is a good life." Thank you for your noble priesthood, your deeper shaman, mister poet.

This book sings more of the Kingdom of God than of the institution of church. It speaks of truth and justice, of moral outrage and the experience of nothingness, of compassion and forgiveness, and it challenges institutional powers that obfuscate and betray and interfere with truth telling. The true Son of God comes preaching the Kingdom of God. At this time in history, the Kingdom of God needs more than ever to take precedence over the institutions of religion whether of church or of football. And so we celebrate the courage and the years it took to remember and to write this book. Out of this remembrance and out of this courage, healing is sure to happen.

William Carlos Williams says that "it is difficult / to get the news from poems / yet men die miserably every day / for lack / of what is found there." Today there are men and women all around the globe who are part of the news of child abuse. This collection of poems, this deep journey into the dark night of the abused soul, can prevent further death and lift some of the misery of the horrible experience of child abuse. These poems invite us to *pray the news,* not just react to it or respond to it with lawyers, media and financial compensation. It takes us to the real hurt, the unspeakable pain by daring to speak the truths that only the soul knows. It will rank, along with the work of John of the Cross, as a truthful telling of what a dark night means as well as what it has to teach us and what the news is telling us. But we owe it to ourselves to read it in the context of the poet's other works, his praise poems, of the blessing that life and existence are and that no one can snuff out.

—Matthew Fox

Prolog: Angel of Power and Protection
Statue on the Bridge to Vatican City, Rome

What happens when the Angel
falls asleep after the mother
and father who held the baby
have to walk back into their lives

and the boy walks out into
the world and a servant
of God molests him when
the parents aren't looking?

By the time he is ready to
cross the bridge to Vatican City
his feet will not move forward
but turn in the opposite direction

and it is decades before he
can approach the old God
by finding his own sacred places
and a new language for praying.

I Counting the Collection

Counting the Collection

Say you are counting
the Sunday collection
with two friends

on Monday afternoon
at the big table
in the back room

when the priest
calls one of you
into his office.

The other two
of you keep counting
the collection

but you both know
what is going on,
you've heard about this,

you know your friend
is sitting on the priest's
lap and squirming,

you hear the sound
of the office chair
on rollers squeak,

you recognize the sounds
of resistance, you know whose
hands have gone where,

you keep counting
the collection, stuffing
coins into wrappers,

stretching rubber bands
around green bills,
adding up totals,

as the squeaking
of the chair
goes on.

Sometime later
your friend comes
back into the room

and nobody looks
at anybody else
and the time has come

to put the money
into the bags,
fill out the deposit

slips, drive to
the bank and come
back to go home

and eat supper with
the sound of a chair
moving and squeaking.

Cleaning the School Boilers

Winter over, the priest
gathers the boys, makes
them crawl inside,

brush off the soot,
like William Blake's
chimney sweeps,

and so of course
the priest feels bad
for the filthy boys,

wants to make them
oh so Spic & Span clean
before they go back home

to Mom and Dad, has
them strip, step into
the hot showers,

soaps his hands.
Guess where they go,
guess where once again

the priest man's
hands go to make
the boys clean.

Boy Scouts

Founder of
the parish Boy
Scout troop,

the priest is always
there for the boys,
taking them on hikes,

taking them fishing,
teaching them about
different trees,

arranging for them
to go camping,
helping them sign up

for summer camp,
but what the priest
cannot stop doing,

as he teaches them
how to uphold
the Boy Scout motto,

what he just cannot
control as he helps
them become more

trustworthy, loyal, helpful,
obedient, cheerful, courteous,
thrifty, brave, clean, reverent,

what he just
cannot stop doing
is putting his irreverent

hands down where
the Boy Scouts all know
they do not belong.

Priest as Hunter

He was a manly man who loved
to hunt pheasants, quail, rabbits,
and squirrels, loved to hunt with dogs,

walk in slowly when a setter was
on the point, flush, shoot, let
the dog bring back the quarry

holding it gently in its mouth,
petted the dog as a reward.
He loved to be out in the fields,

he loved to be out in the woods,
in the open air, to hunt
with his brothers

and brothers-in-law, listen to
the beagles bring around an old
buck rabbit as wily as the hills,

rejoiced and gave praise when
a relative got the shot and the kill.
Sometimes he brought along

boys who wanted to learn
how to hunt, and after his
brothers and brothers-in-law

went home for the night,
he taught the apprentice hunters
what it means to be the hunted.

Catholic Boy Blues I

Where the priest's hands always want to go?
Why they always have to go where they go?
Please Mama, please Papa, tell me it isn't so.

How can a priest say one thing and do another?
What's it like to preach one thing and do another?
How can he do that to me and be somebody's brother?

How can a man like that look anyone in the eye?
How can a priest like that look anyone in the eye
without turning his whole life into a big fat lie?

Voice in the Vestibule

What's the matter, boy?
Cat got your tongue?
Priest got your penis?

Where Is Jesus?

Where is Jesus
when a priest
gropes boys?

What would Jesus do?
What would Jesus say?

Would he turn the other cheek,
be a lamb, mild and meek,
be quick to forgive,
insist you find a better way to live?

Or would he turn into a lion and roar,
as he throws you out the door,
Thou shalt not defile My Father's house?

Tell me, priest,
tell me true,
does it make you blue?

Where is Jesus
when you do
what you do?

If My Poor Parents

If my poor father had known
what his friend, confessor,
and spiritual advisor the priest

had done to his son and others,
would his nerves have unraveled
and had to be put back together

by the shock of electricity yet
another time? Would my father's
"scrupulosity" have been triggered

all over again, making him feel
he had done something wrong
as a father to allow such a thing

to happen and guarantee
that he himself could never be
forgiven and his soul was therefore

damned for all eternity? If the priest
could have understood what he was
causing his fragile friend to suffer,

would he have tried to gain control
of his hands and whatever drove them
to do what they did, if only to stop

my father from plunging into depression
and despair of salvation with no hope
of rising again, with or without help?

* * * *

If my mother had known
what her pastor had done

and continued to do
while she invited him

into her home and served
him food she cooked

for her family, what would
she have said and done,

how would she have explained
to the younger brothers and sister?

Each and every time
the priest came into her presence

where would she have put her eyes
without the right words to say?

Deathbed Story

Got me a brother be gone.
Not dead but way gone.
Mama told me this story
when she was barely alive.

Breathing hard from a tank,
she sat up in her recliner
and told me with a sad voice
that implied more than it said,

told me my brother he went
into the seminary to serve God,
but he soon knew it wasn't right
for him to be and stay there.

He knew he had to stop
and told this to the priest
who helped pay his tuition.
The priest he got real angry

and said, Boy, you don't stay
till end of the first full year
you won't become an Eagle
Scout like your big brother is.

So he had to stay and it
ate him alive and ever
since then he rebelled
against the whole place

and got the creeps in church.
Every sermon he heard
about doing the right thing
cut deep into his heart.

This pain grew worse
and he did not want
to come home ever again
and began to slip away

from his brothers, his sister,
sister-in-law, nieces and nephews,
but our mother, who told this story
in a ghostly voice, did not understand

on her deathbed, or did she see,
before she slipped away, why
he would have to go and stay
away from us forever. Did she?

My Father's Wake

When he appeared
at my father's wake
from the country parish

where he became pastor,
nine years after I
moved far away,

I introduced him
to my wife. He looked
at my full black beard,

blushed, the only
confession I ever
saw him make

on his side of the curtain,
and said, in a kind
of mock country gruffness,

"Well, I never thought
you would stay anywhere
that long!" Right, I could

never have stayed anywhere
I'd have to endure your masquerade
and your hectoring voice.

But nine years in the East
turned into thirty-four.
Some twenty years after

you were embalmed
and laid out as my
father was that night,

I moved back to Indiana,
but not to my hometown.
Too many boys see a ghost

clad in black and white collar when
they return there to visit family.
You became the Monsignor

Molester the boys,
now men and fathers,
carry in their heads

when they go to church,
if they ever enter one.
You are the ghost corpse

I must talk back to,
in any voice I can
find, to exorcise.

Whose Confession?

Back home from college
on summer vacation,
I decide to go to confession.

I'm the only parishioner
in the church, he's the only
priest in the confessional.

When I tell him I have
not been going to Sunday
mass, for reasons I feel

no obligation to give,
he becomes angry, says:
You can't do that!

The Hand

The hand that reaches
for the altar boy's crotch

rubs oil on the fore-
head of the dying.

The hand that fondles a boy
making him go erect

blesses and baptizes
the new-born babe.

The hand that pulls a boy's
hand onto his man penis

consecrates the union
of a man and a woman.

Not Even Isaiah and Jeremiah

Not even the great
visionary wordsmiths
Isaiah and Jeremiah

had to find words
to tell their people
how it feels

for a boy
to be so defiled
by a priest

that for fifty years
he keeps his mouth shut
even to those he loves.

Where Was God?

The priest was God
and God knew what
he was doing,
what he could
get away with,
why no one
could touch him.

God knew when
the nuns would be
gone from the building,
he knew every corner
and stairs in the school,
every sound and shadow
and ray of light,
knew every coming
and going in his web.

God was big and great
the boys were small
and powerless, their parents
did not know,
nobody could tell,
nobody had invented
the right language to
to get across to adults
what God was doing
to the boys.

So God was there
when it all happened,
and everybody believed

in God, everybody
worshiped God,
God was the center
of their universe.

Yes, God got the boys
and sometimes they whispered
to one another about
what was happening,
but to no one else.

God walked away
and God was praised
and received a promotion
to the rank of Monsignor
and God was good
and God was respected
and God rewarded
those who were faithful
and blessed them all.

The Piety of a Pedophile

The priest arranges
for two boys
to spend the night

in his bedroom
so they can serve
his early mass.

Which one will
sleep on ice
with a priest's

hand groping
his crotch
and which one

will awaken in
the night to find
the priest standing

beside his bed
reaching down
to insert prowling

fingers inside
the slit of
junior briefs?

In the morning
when the priest
asks him if he wants

to go to confession
before the low
mass begins

the boy wearing
yellowed briefs voices
a vehement *No!*

Both boys feel
slimy as they slither
down the steps

from the bedroom
into the sacristy,
slip white surplices

over black robes,
pour water and wine,
ring the bell.

They stare at
the priest as he
elevates the Host

before the congregation
with the piety
of a pedophile

squinting up into
the darkened eyes
of an all-seeing God.

Confiteor Deo

Confiteor Deo Omnipotente,
Confiteor Deo Omnipotente,

I confess to Almighty God,
I confess to Almighty God,

that I took a young boy,
yes I took a young boy

who wanted to serve at mass,
who wanted to serve at mass

and made him memorize prayers in Latin,
and made him memorize his prayers in Latin,

had him recite those prayers to me,
had him recite those prayers to me,

to prove he was worthy to serve,
to prove he was worthy to serve,

and while he was learning to pray in Latin,
yes, while he was learning to pray in Latin,

I let my hands go where they should not have gone,
I let my hands go where they should never have gone,

I admit to all I touched that poor boy wrong,
I admit to all I touched that poor boy wrong

Confiteor Deo Omnipotente,
Confiteor Deo Omnipotente,

I confess to Almighty God,
I confess to Almighty God,

first I made a boy pray to You in Latin,
first I made a boy pray to You in Latin,

then I touched him in a foreign language,
then I touched him in a foreign language

no human being should ever have to learn,
no human being should ever have to learn.

To Dorothy Day

Catholic worker Dorothy Day,
what would you say

to the kind of priest
who makes a feast

of young boys
he treats as toys

and when they grow older
becomes even bolder

as he walks calmly away
toward the brand new day

when younger ones come
he can play like a drum?

To Hildegard of Bingen

Dear medieval mystic,
dear maker of music,
creator of canticles of ecstasy,
crafter of poems of praise
to the beauty of Creation,
dear visionary who saw
the inter-relationships among
all things that live
and are therefore holy,

help me understand,
help me see,
help me move beyond
any blot and blotch
that stains this world.

Dear sweet sister in song
and poem and hymn,
dear devotee of the word,
dear seer into the divine,
help me find light
after the heavy darkness
that settled on my soul
after I admitted to myself
the shepherd's attacks
on me and others.

To Mechthild of Magdeburg

Dear Mechthild of Magdeburg,
may you whose soul spoke
to God as your lover,

you who longed for God,
who asked Him
to lead you in a dance

and help you leap
into love and then
into knowledge and go

beyond human sense,
upon whose soul
God descended

like dew on a flower;
may you, passionate mystic,
help me find a way still

to venerate the God
whose ordained servant
became so vile,
so repugnant

that afterwards
the mere mention
of the word love

made the boy I was
hang his head
and hope that sleep

could somehow
bring back sun
to shine again.

To Isaiah

Isaiah, my hero, I wake in the middle
of the night again thinking of how an angel

of God came to you and put burning coals
to your lips to purify you and make you ready

to receive the holy words and let them come
through you in flame and thunderbolt them

on to us so we might mend our ways and see
lightning flash and hear thunder crack to bring us

out of the wilderness of blue darkness we feel
pressing down on us. Since I admitted to myself

what another servant of God did to me and others
when we were boys, I have often felt burning

in my gut embers that are hottest at night.
I awaken over and over to ask your help

to make me strong and keep me telling
this bitter truth that hurts so bad.

Isaiah, my inspiration, be there for me,
stay, stay with me all the way. Help me

show others that violating the truth
when we tell others they must live it

is an abomination against our God.
Oh my ancient father, my seer, my sayer,

give me the strength to bear up, carry on,
and speak out for others who suffer abuse.

Oh batter my heart but lift my soul,
man of red-hot words. Give me courage.

Give me spirit. Give me spunk. Fan my
flame to burn high in this dark night.

Catholic Boy Blues II

Blues, you know you can't stay away from me.
Blues, anybody can see you want to be with me.
If I make you my friend, maybe I can go free!

Blues, if you can't go away and let me be,
Blues, if you can't up and go and let me be,
maybe I should just make you a part of me.

Priest, I can see you'll never go far away.
Priest, I can see you'll never be far away.
If you're gone at night, you return in the day.

Blues, teach me how to see through my tears.
Blues, teach me how to get beyond my tears.
To welcome you took me so many years!

Priest, maybe I should settle for having my say.
Priest, maybe I should be glad to have my say.
The road to forgive runs such a long, long way.

Blues, my old buddy, I admit I do love you.
Singing you has helped me find what's true.
Singing you has helped me say what's true.

To Some Blues Mamas and Papas

Robert Johnson, teach me how to make
a deal and save my soul at the crossroads.

Bessie Smith, show me how to tell folks
it ain't nobody's business what I do or say.

Son House, bottleneck me to a quiet place
where I can forgive and bless my abuser.

Muddy Waters, get your mojo goin'
so I can put a gris-gris on evil spirits.

John Lee Hooker, boogie woogie me to stomp
my boot heel on the head of Old King Snake.

Charley Patton, help me rise to the top and swim
on the surface of the waters flooding my soul.

Rev. Gary Davis, pray for me, pray for me,
so I can bypass those who trespass against me.

Sister Rosetta Thorpe, gospel me into the air
leading beyond into a heaven somewhere.

I Saw My Father

I saw my father
in his rocking chair
again rocking back

and forth in silent
tears as I remember
him rocking that time

he came back from
our Lady of the Peace
where he suffered

shock treatment,
but this time
the shock was

different. He was
crying for what
you his friend

did to me his son.
I wanted to take
him in my arms

and say, Dad,
I am so sorry,
this will pass.

Let us try
to forgive him
no matter how

wretched the thing
that he did.
He must not

have known how
vile his offence,
must not have

been able to choke
off his impulse.
He must have

been too sick
to get help.
He had to have

known the wrong
he did and felt
the pain he caused.

Surely he knew
he would one day
have to atone.

Don't cry, Dad.
I am so sorry.
Please don't cry.

Catholic Boy Blues III

Robert Johnson said come on in my kitchen.
Outside the rain's goin' to come down pitchin'.
Come back in my kitchen and be my religion.

I too was standing out in acid rain.
Too long I was left out in the rain
where I felt a burning scalding pain.

Back in the kitchen, Mama's at the stove.
Back in the kitchen, Mama's at the stove
cooking up a big batch of country love.

Priest, you still standing out in the rain.
I see you still standing out in the rain.
You gotta be feeling some kind of pain.

My mama done fed you before,
she done fed you her food before,
now she might not open the door.

Priest, my best advice is to pray.
Priest, I got to tell you go pray.
What else can a boy like me say?

You better listen for the song of the dove.
Maybe you get lucky, find some kinda love.
Could take a miracle to bring you right love.

Catholic Boy Blues IV

Mr. Blues, I've grown cozy with you.
Mr. Blues, now I'm so cozy with you
there's something I'd really like to do.

You know all about my misery.
You know all about my misery
and you can help me set it free.

I want my friends to come over here.
I'll invite my friends to come over here.
We'll sit around and sip some cold beer.

You play and sing, Mr. Blues, you do that.
You play and sing, Mr. Blues, you do that
while you wearin' a funky old baseball hat.

You help me tell my sorry story.
If you help me tell my sorry story
you and I can move on toward glory.

With a friend like you right there,
with a friend like you in the chair
I know it's alright for me to share

this never-ending tale of a song
that will help this boy be strong
and maybe right his tale of wrong.

Catholic Boy Blues V

Blues, I got another gig for you.
Blues, I got another job for you
but it ain't nothin' you cain't do.

There's this priest you heard about.
There's this priest you heard about.
Word is he might be down and out.

I'd love for him to hear you play.
I'd love for him to hear you play.
Don't matter if it's night or day.

Play him a blues low down and slow.
Play him a gut-bucket blues real slow.
Let's see where that makes him go.

We both know blues are good for the soul.
You might even make a sorry priest whole.
You might even save his mother-lovin' soul.

Catholic Boy Blues VI

I got a spiritual advisor who's a woman.
Priest, if you can't listen to any woman
this boy got to call you an ol' Chauvin.

Priest, why don't you just let it go?
Can't you be bigger and let it go?
Why you want to stay down low?

Don't you think it's time to rise?
Why don't you just up and rise?
Listen to women, folks say you wise!

Around here we like our priests modest.
For us, God's servant got to be modest.
Worst thing he could ever be is a sadist.

Stop fightin' and let yourself give in.
Stop fightin' and let yourself listen.
If you do, I know you gonna win.

Catholic Boy Blues VII

Priest, I got to move on down the road.
Priest, I got to mosey on down the road.
Looks like you still carryin' a big load.

Mr. Blues, you know you're comin' along.
Yeah, baby, you sure be comin' along.
You showed me how to sing this song.

Sister Advisor, you know I'll stay in touch.
Sister Advisor, you know I'll stay in touch.
This boy says thanks for helping so much.

Reader, thanks for coming along with me.
Thanks for coming down this road with me.
I hope I may have helped you see

that there's great strength in a song,
that there's mighty mojo in a song
when we all learn how to sing along.

II The Boy and the Man He Became

Childhood Lessons

Back then I was in touch
with animals that crawled
into thickets or slept
in holes in trees.

Bird song was a music
that came to me clearly,
as if amplified by
a special sound system.

But I also saw up close
the darkness of a man,
supposedly holy, who could
not stop putting his hungry

hands where they had
no right to go. From this
man who wore the collar
and listened to others

tell him their sins,
I learned what it meant
to be the hunted, not
just an apprentice hunter.

From him I learned that
the touch of God's representative
on earth respected no boundaries
and defiled the Holy Word.

Prayer for Survivors

May we come to see and accept
that we had no means whatsoever
then to say no to the man
who held the holy hammer.

May we come to understand
that today we have the voice
and vision to speak out
against the wrongs done to us.

May we find the power
to condemn the betrayal
forced on us so others
will not suffer humiliation.

May we discover the strength,
may we be given the courage,
may we come into the power
of words to expose the charade

of religious authority figures
who proclaim one set of values
and vision from on high, in the pulpit,
but put into practice the opposite

by taking advantage of the innocent
who have no recourse but to accept
what is done to them because no one
would believe what they try to say.

May we refuse to think
that we were abused and defiled
because we did something
we should not have done.

May we transform the pain
and the shame we have known
into the energy and might
that will help save others.

Give us wisdom, give us strength,
give us the ability and the will
to stand up and testify against
the wrongs of the past so that

they will not be repeated in the present.
Let our anger fuel our fight to help
those who have not yet come
to understand what was done to them.

Let us forgive but never forget.
Let us open the eyes of those
who could not believe what
we said we had to endure.

Breakdown Blues

Papa broke down every once in a while.
It started when he lost his smile.
He came apart every once in a while.

We all turned quiet and a little sad.
We weren't mad, just little kid sad.
If your papa hurts, you're never glad.

Papa, he would go talk to the priest.
Papa, he took himself to see the priest.
He wanted to get some advice at least.

When they took our papa away,
after they drove him away
Mama did once upon a time say:

Son, we can do it, you will see.
Believe me, we can do it, you'll see.
Now you're the man of the family.

Mr. Blues, for so long you been my good friend,
for a very long time you been my best friend.
Your kind of friendship will never end.

I'll always bring you along wherever I go,
a friend like you comes wherever I go
to help me climb up when I feel low.

Deputy Blues

Mr. Blues, I hereby make you my deputy.
My Old Friend, I appoint you my deputy.
I would also ask you to be my emissary.

When you're out singin' on the road,
when you're out strummin' on the road,
I ask you to carry some of my heavy load.

You sing so well you'll come to the pearly gate.
Your immortal song will bring you to that gate,
and when you arrive, if it's not already too late,

if you find my mama and papa inside,
if you happen to find them reunited inside,
play them a country blues, take them aside

and ask if they know anything about that man,
please ask if they may have seen that man
who took advantage of their boy and ran.

If they know where this priest resides,
if they know where this man now resides,
send him a message to leave where he hides.

Tell him it's past time to make amends,
tell him I'm old and he should make amends,
tell him that if he would relent and send

my angry, hurt, and lost brother back to me,
if he can find him and send him back to me,
I'll release this crippling curse and set him free.

Stained Soul Blues

Wherever my papa may now be,
wherever our papa may now be,
I hope he can see crystal clear

how that man we called a priest,
how that man said he was a priest
was just about the very least

help any man could ever be,
worst help any man could be,
'cause of what he did to me.

What he did to me and my brethren,,
did to me and my poor parish brethren
might block him from entering heaven.

That priest man did not do us right,
naw, he did not do much that was right.
He took our innocence in the night

and next morning he put on the stole,
very next morning he put on the stole
and stained his immortal soul.

The Hurt Heart Says

I got this hurt in my heart,
got this old hurt in my heart
wakes me after giving me a start.

Son, you got to find your voice
yeah, you got to find your voice,
hurt heart says, you got no choice

but to help others begin to see,
got to show others how to see,
that the pain and the misery

you older boys have felt so long,
the heavy hurt you felt so long,
can help you right the wrong

that was done to others, too,
done to many others, too,
not just you, not just you.

Mr. Blues, I hear you in my heart.
Old friend, you're down in my heart
and you're kind to help me start

finding out whatever I can do,
to learn what a writer can do,
to lift folks up from being blue.

Let It Rip

Once upon a time there was a boy.
There was this polite and gentle boy
got manhandled and lost his joy.

But this boy could not be kept down.
Though a priest forced him to frown
this boy would not be held down.

If you are familiar with this story,
if this is also your very own story,
declare it as part of church history.

It's time for you, too, to come out.
It's time you and you also come out.
Let our whispers be reborn as a shout.

It's past time to step out and let it rip.
Show some cheek, yeah, give some lip.
Join your brothers and sisters: let it rip.

Jesus Seer and Sayer

Help me see what to say and do.
Let me see like you what I must do
to help others by saying like you.

I love you as a young rebel
when you overturned the table.
I love you most as a rebel.

Tell me your powerful secrets.
Tell me you had no regrets
in living the word of the prophets.

I love Isaiah and Jeremiah,
my heroes Jeremiah and Isaiah,
but prophets end up as pariahs

for telling a heavy and hard truth.
They die telling an unpopular truth
that can't be told by a green youth.

I didn't face this truth until I was old,
couldn't face this truth until I grew old,
didn't know how to forge a language bold

enough to expose one of your servants.
Could not accuse one of your servants,
question his reputation, serve a warrant

that charged he did not serve You.
I know that man did not serve You.
Help me say it straight and true.

Mr. Blues Says Thanks

Man, I'm so glad to hear what you say.
Glad you have your say in your own way.
Singing the dirty blues brings a better day.

My man, you know what I like?
Let me tell you what I really like.
I like the way you suck it up and strike

out to help other boys who were hurt.
Yessir, help all the others who got hurt.
A man like you got to sound the alert

so other boys now turned into men,
other boys who also are grown men
can look inside of themselves. When

they are ready to take a stand,
are ready to rise up and stand,
you be there to understand

how hard it is to tell a hurtful truth,
so hard to tell the dirty, awful truth
of what happened to you as a youth.

Yeah, man, I admire and respect you for that.
It's easy for me to listen and relate to that.
Sometimes I feel like a helpless gnat,

but when I stand up and sing the blues,
standing up and singing the country blues
feels good down to the holes in my shoes.

Mr. Blues and Etheridge Knight

It's always up and down, as you know.
Sometimes up, sometimes down, bro.
Mr. Blues, I still refuse to give up though.

Got to pull yourself up again by the bootstrap.
Better pull yourself up again by the bootstrap
if you don't want to be caught in a nasty trap.

Mr. Blues, you always a free singer be.
My friend, you always a free singer be.
Like Etheridge, you got the power to see.

Old Etheridge, he got thrown into the clink.
Pre-poet Etheridge got thrown into the clink
as his life stumbled and teetered on the brink,

but behind bars he was released into his own voice,
he became the man reborn in a powerful voice
that spoke for down and outs with little choice.

Brother Etheridge spoke from the country of the heart,
he taught himself to write from the center of his heart:
the spoken language of head and heart was his art.

Mr. Blues, you and Etheridge close brothers be.
Mr. Blues, you and Etheridge bosom buddies be.
Etheridge's blues came to Indiana from Mississippi

and he sang the blues for you and me.
Oh yeah, he sang the blues for you and me.
Now Etheridge Knight sings for all eternity.

The Boy to the Man He Became

I know you had to leave me
behind to make a good life.

Had to keep moving on
and not look back at little me

too often or too long
so you could survive.

Not think of what he did to me
to spare yourself the misery.

But did you ever wonder
what it was like for me

to be left all alone by myself
sitting in my filthy little corner

on my pretty little stool
as the holy man would drool?

Nobody to speak to me
or for me, nobody to see

where his hot hands went,
nobody to help me vent.

To have surrendered my say.
To have given up my play.

Not to have any voice.
Not to have any choice.

To be left all alone
sore to the bone.

Keeping Clean

When I would keep
my eye on the ball

to hit it hard
was I not

smashing him
in the face?

When I would
shoot the ball

through the hoop
so hard it

would slash
and rip the net

was I not
slapping his face?

When I would
flush the toilet

and watch a turd
swirl down and away

was I not trying
to get rid of him?

Mystery

In what class
in the seminary

or what book
of the holy Bible

did the man
bending over

the bed
of the boy

in the dark
learn so well

how to work
his fingers

inside the slot
of the briefs

to find what
he craved

to touch
and turn hard?

The Man to the Boy He Was

A poet once said the child
is father to the man so I

write to express to my child
father my heartfelt thanks

for the blessings you gave
to the man he became.

You gave him the bounty
of rolling woods and fields,

a taste for the fruits of black
walnut and shagbark hickory.

Introduced him to the habits
of wily fox and wild gray squirrels,

the bounding of cottontails,
the soaring of red-tail hawks.

Showed him the plain and plentiful
beauty of wild carrot and broom sedge,

the thrill of pulling catfish, bluegill
and crappie out of local waters.

Attuned his ears to the bob bob white
cry of the quail and the explosion

as a covey breaks into flight.
You gave him a love of baseball,

football, basketball, hiking along
rock roads, farm lanes, trails

through fields and woods, past
lakes and rivers. Taught him

the magic of reading books that
opened up worlds he never knew.

Passed on a love of the sounds
of words and the rhythms of music

that have given him the capacity
to say as he looks back now:

Thanks, despite the priest,
for birthing the man he is.

Mr. Blues Calls Time Out

Whooie, just what's goin' on over here?
I call time to ask what's goin' down here.
I got to think and say it ain't at all clear.

Please, Lord, let me get this straight.
Please, Lord, somebody set me straight
before the devil fly on over to investigate.

Once upon a time there was this boy,
once upon a time there was this boy,
lecherous goat priest done stole his joy.

Okay, the man that boy went and became,
the man that poor boy went and became,
wakes up to himself pretty late in the game.

Then the man he became wrote to the boy he was,
this older man wrote to the boy he back then was.
To make himself heal and become whole he says:

Thanks, boy, thanks, son, for all you done;
Thanks, boy, father-boy, for all you done.
That priest sure was one sick son of a gun!

Right about then through the back door in I walks.
Right about then through the back door in I walks
Pickin' and strummin' my old guitar like it talks.

But the boy and the man and Mr. Blues are one.
This boy and this man and Mr. Blues are all one.
Somebody somewhere got to be putting me on!

To see it and say it and sing it like this,
Lord almighty, what a crazy story this is!
A book as messed up as this cain't miss!

Come with Me

Come with me into the woods.
We'll lose ourselves in the ravines,

give our energies to climbing
the hilltops, look down from ridges.

We'll find ourselves delightfully lost
in the hollows, meander with the creeks.

We'll look all the way up to the tops
of shagbark hickories and tulip poplars,

towering way beyond our limits.
We'll step down the sides of slopes

and marvel at the green of Christmas
ferns unfurling out of dry brown leaves.

Wherever we look, whatever
we hear, whatever we feel,

there will be no predator priest
behind us when we pause to rest.

Mr. Blues' Appreciation

Man, you ain't a boy no more.
Man, you ain't no boy no more.
You about done evened the score.

You came on out of the dark.
You came right out of the dark,
came out of range of the shark.

Any boy who can sing his song,
any boy who can sing his song
like you sang your song is strong.

What I say is you're now a man.
It's plain to see you're now a man.
You sing it as good as any man can.

Son, I'm proud to call you my friend.
Yes sir, proud to call you my friend.
You got the gift to mend and fend

all for yourself and other people too.
You help yourself and other people too.
I got to say you be a blues man true!

Symptoms

Did you ever wonder
why you always notice

so many frowns,
hear so many sighs,

relate to so many people
down on their luck,

want to speak out
against so much injustice,

so often feel
so easily betrayed,

take on so many burdens,
right so many wrongs,

want to help so many people,
feel responsible for what

life has done to so many—
but do not take the steps

that will help you see
you should be kinder

and more respectful to
the person you are

and appreciate the good
you have done?

Success Story

Never did a priest
succeed so well

at making a boy
ache for a girl.

The Boy Asks the Man He Became

It must have been hard,
when you moved far away,
to remember once in a while
what happened way back then.

Could you tell our father?
Could you tell our mother?
What about our brothers and sister,
though they were younger?

And what about our friends,
as they grew older and wiser?
Did you ever try to tell them?
Ask if maybe one of them, too?

It must have been so hard
to keep me locked in the closet.
It must have been as hard
for you as it was for me.

Was it ever hard to breathe?
Did you ever tell your wife?
Did you ever tell your children?
Were you ever not able to pray?

Did the priest ever come back
after you thought you put him behind?
Did you ever come to understand
why you had to get out of town?

Did you realize why you drank so much?
Did you see that you came back home
so often as a way of telling me you
knew I was still there waiting for you?

A Boy's Post Script

For so long I realized
I could see before you did
that you would one day
have to turn and look back.

Not only would you have to
look back, but come back,
to the place you loved so
much even though it hurt you.

I knew you would come back
and open your eyes to me
because you kept coming back
to the scenes I never left.

In a way, you never left.
If I stayed, you were here.
I stayed here all the time,
but also came with you.

I know this is a lot
for you to comprehend,
but I knew you would come
home when the time was right.

You had to survive.
You had to make a life.
You had to be ready.
I knew you would do it.

I never gave up faith.
I never became impatient.
I knew how to forgive.
And now you're back!

The Way into the Woods

For years I knew I had
to get back into the woods,
but did not know if I could.
Could not tell if I ever would.

Could not find the way back.
The woods were not on a map.
No one could tell me how
I might find the way.

One day I awoke and found
my feet were carrying me
in what I knew was the right
direction though I could not see.

This poem is taking me there,
bringing you along with me,
toward the center of the woods,
toward whatever I must find.

We will arrive together,
then work out how to get
back out of these woods,
which are dark and deep.

The deeper we go, the more
we shall see; the more
we lose, the more we shall
find, walking together.

We are now entering a cave.
We are now standing in water.
Do not, do not be afraid.
This is the water that heals.

Mr. Blues Intervenes

Here's something I have to say.
I ain't got no choice but to say:
Man, what a price you pay!

My friend, please don't forget,
this thing ain't all over just yet!
Don't ever let yourself forget.

My man, don't tear yourself apart.
Don't keep on ripping yourself apart.
Listen to the message of your heart.

There is something I ask you to start.
Something helpful I ask you to start:
Have mercy on your poor heavy heart.

I know it ain't easy to let it all go
but if you do your heart will grow.
You proved it ain't easy to let go.

Don't let a tender heart grow hard.
Don't let a merciful heart grow hard.
Don't turn your soul into a brittle shard.

You bet I know you and yours been hurt bad.
Your blues brother knows you been hurt bad,
but sing your blues and you won't stay sad.

Ode to No

If Ludwig van Beethoven
had known what the priest did,
for the choral movement
of his Ninth Symphony,
he would have composed
an "Ode to No."

If Johnnie Cash had known,
he would have walked the No line
and made that priest go down
into a burning ring of No.

If Elvis Presley had known,
he would have shook his hips
and sung with a surly lip,
"You ain't nothin'
but a No, No, No!"

If the Everly Brothers of Kentucky
had known what the priest did,
they would have sung,
in their heavenly harmony,
"All I have to do
is dream No, No, No."

If little Bobbie Zimmerman
out of Hibbing, Minnesota
had known when he left town
and went on the road
to write his own songs,
he would have asked,
"How many roads
must a boy walk down
before he can say No?"

If Paul, John, George and Ringo
had known what the priest did,
their refrain would have been,
"All you need is No,
No is all you need."

If Emily Dickinson had known,
she would have left behind
in her dresser drawer
a short anthem for all victims:
"Success is counted sweetest
by those who have no power
but somehow find a way
to say No, No, No!"

If Robert Frost had known,
he would have pondered
at his midnight desk
and concluded the poem
so many people have loved,
"But I have miles to go
before I can say No,
so many miles to go
before I can say No!"

Mr. Blues Sings Yes

Comes to me somethin' a good friend ought to suggest.
Comes to me somethin' this good friend ought to suggest.
You can say that No, but boy you got to live the Yes.

I 'member the night your Cajun wife cooked crawfish stew.
I 'member the night your Cajun wife cooked crawfish stew.
She made a brown roux and a pot of yellow corn maque choux.

Up stood your little Colombian girl to play some cool fiddle.
Up stood your little Colombian girl to play some cool fiddle.
When you want good food and music, you right in the middle!

Up stood your little Colombian boy and played some hot guitar.
Up stood your little Colombian boy and played some hot guitar.
When you want good food and music, you don't have to go far!

Okay, you got some mean and nasty stuff in your past.
I admit you got some mean and nasty stuff in your past.
My mama used to say, "Son, let go of that bitter sass!"

When you feel bad, sing the blues and you feel good.
When you feel bad, sing the blues and you feel good.
Pretty soon you see good folks in your neighborhood.

From where I stand, I see the bad but you also been blessed.
From where I stand, I see the bad but you also been blessed.
You can say and sing the No, but boy you got to live the Yes!

These Thy gifts

Mama's in the kitchen
cooking up a roast.
Daddy's in the basement
siphoning sweet wine
to drink with the guest.
Priest's on his way over
for another free meal.
Boys come to the table,
fold young hands and pray.
Little sis sits babbling
in her wooden high chair.
Priest raises his right hand,
the one he can't control,
and blesses the food.
Everybody chows down.
Soon Daddy will be taken
away for shock treatment
and Mama will pray hard.
Priest will help the family
that prays together stay
together by helping himself
to little boy flesh.
Bless us oh Lord
and these thy gifts,
amen, amen, amen.

Navajo Crucifix

On a pawn table
inside a museum
I saw an old

silver crucifix
with turquoise stones
 I would have

loved to polish
and wear on a chain;
but I knew the pain

that beautiful cross
would bring back
from when I was a boy

would burn a stigmata
on my heart that
would never go away.

Once Upon a Time a Boy

in another family in our parish
was abused by the same priest
you have been reading about
and it messed him up bad.

After so many times.
the boy got up his nerve
and told his daddy what
that priest did to him.
He was hoping for help,
but his daddy hauled off
and beat the shit out of him.
This messed him up more.

When the boy got older
they sent him to 'Nam
and messed him up even more.
He was taught to kill
for democracy and saw
his buddies die after their blood
splattered onto his hands.

Once upon a time
this boy who had been
abused by a priest
came back home to his parish
in the hills of southern Indiana
from the killing fields of Asia,
with anger in his heart
and hurt on his hands.

This young man who learned
how to take another man's life
later told a friend, "I should have
killed that SOB right then and there.
I knew how to do it and could have
saved some of our little brothers."

More Catholic Boy Blues

I got them old Catholic boy blues,
got a mess of Catholic boy blues.
In my house the blues always rules.

Sometimes it gets a little bit better,
Sometimes I feel a little bit better,
then the bottom falls out of the weather.

Only way to come all the way through,
only way to come all the way through
is to tell it straight and tell it true,

be faithful to what I feel and see,
be faithful to what I feel and see,
hope and pray peace finds me

so I can share it with you,
so I can share it with you,
help you do what you gotta do.

Weary Confession

There is a hole
in my stomach
no words can repair,

a hurt in my heart
no liturgy
can alleviate,

and a tear
in my spirit no
ceremony can heal.

Numbers in the Wind

How many boys were there,
you want to know?
You say tell it square?
How many boys did
that priest man molest?
Who will blow off the lid?

Who among us really knows?
What's the Bishop say?
Does he count by fours?
Does he count by fives?
What's all this jive?
Or does he count by three?
A trinity in one family.
Second in yet another.

That's already six—
pretty many dirty tricks.
Would you say only ten
over all those years?
No bigger numbers in your pen?
Afraid of the people's fears?
How big will the numbers grow?
You think it could not be so?

How many boys were there,
you want to know?
Watch the numbers grow.
You think asking is not fair?
How many times the priest sinned?
Might as well go listen to the wind.

Mr. Blues on Red-Hot Spleen

Boy, you sure got some red-hot spleen,
yessir, you sure got some red-hot spleen.
For you, ain't no maybe, no in between.

Anybody can see you got to get all the truth out.
Anybody can see you got to get the whole truth out.
Go on, go on, if you got to, boy, go on and shout!

Listen, I still be here when you come back.
Mr. Blues still be here when you come back.
So long the road, so many curves in the track.

I'll remember you each and every one of my days,
always 'member you every single one of my days.
Mr. Blues stands by whatever his young friend says.

Mr. Blues knows where you're comin' from.
Mr. Blues can see where you're comin' from.
Nobody who knows him could call him dumb.

He sees you got to go and stand in this storm.
He sees you got to go and steer through this storm.
For you he stays in and keeps the home fires warm.

The Dirty Little Secret

Why'd you have to spoil it
for everybody else?
Why could you not keep
your dirty little secret
to yourself? How hard
would that have been?
Why, why, why did you
have to tell it to the world?

Wasn't he our pastor?
Didn't he found the parish?
Didn't he do us all good?
Was he really all that bad?
Didn't he build up the Boy Scouts?
Didn't he support all sports?
Don't you agree he helped
bring in St. Vincent DePaul?
Didn't you like the turkey shoot?
Didn't you enjoy the parish picnic?
Didn't you appreciate it when
he came into each classroom
to give out all the report cards?
What's wrong with you?
Didn't he help make you
one of our Eagle Scouts?

Why you want to make
us all look so bad?
What's the point of exploding
this story fifty years later?
What good will this do?

Is this what we need now?
Don't you know this town
is rated one of the best places
in the whole country to live?
Don't you know our ratings
might drop way low?
Why'd you have to spoil it
for everybody else?

Why talk about what this did to you?
Why go on about what this did
to your brothers and sisters?
Why bring your wife into the story
and your children and maybe
your grandchildren? Why imagine
what this would have done
to your parents if they had known?
Why must this be our problem?
Why rub our faces in it?

So what if we did know?
So what if we passed around
the dirty little secret
in the cafeteria and classroom
and on the playground
and thought about it when
he said the mass and gave
the Sunday sermon as we
sat there in our little suits
and ties and taffeta dresses?
So what if he went after
one of our brothers
or one of our cousins
or one of our neighbors?
Do you think we didn't care?

Aren't we all in this together?
Shouldn't we have kept it to ourselves?
Aren't we all good German Catholics?
What good can this possibly do?
Who says we should pay this price?
Who says it's our fault a man
we looked up to and revered
did this to all of us and ours?
Why should we have to think about
how we could all let this happen?
Wasn't he one of us?

Are you so desperate to find
something sordid to write about?
I like it better when you keep
telling the story of our ancestors
and sing the praises of our hills
and our woods and our fields.
Why'd you have to do this
to yourself and everybody else?

Dialogue Between the Man and the Boy

Where did the boy
I was have to go
when I left town?

Right where you
left me, all
by myself.

How did it feel
to be so all
alone so long?

Thanks for asking,
sometimes I thought
you never would.

So sorry I
could not be
more attentive.

That's okay, I
love the place but
not the loneliness.

Must have been
hard to think
nobody knew.

Not really. So
many people did
know deep down.

But didn't it
hurt you that no-
body spoke out?

Yes, but sometimes
boys must be
more mature,

more understanding,
and more patient
than their elders.

If

If his bird dogs
Queenie and Ike
that our family kept
in a pen in the woods
loved him so much,
he must have been
at least partly good.

If so many mothers
and fathers looked
up to him for so long,
he must have done
something good
for the community.

If he spent so many
hours arranging for
Boy Scouts to work
on merit badges
and climb toward
the ultimate Eagle,
he could not have
been all bad.

If he took boys
into the woods
and fields to
instruct them on
how to develop
the right values to
become good hunters,
he must have had
some higher purpose.

If he gave his life
to serving God
and His people,
he must have
felt some goodness
in himself he hoped
to share with parishioners.

If he took vows
and read the Bible
and did daily devotions
and said the mass
and gave out communion,
surely something inside
himself must have
suffered terribly, must
have eaten away at him
when he did to us boys
what he had to know
was deep down hideous.

Kid, Kid

Kid, kid, don't ever give up on me.
I went away but not so far as you think.
You still got a lot to say to me, I can see.

Kid, I tell you it was nothing you did,
nothing you made happen or could control.
How hard it must have been to keep it hid!

Please don't feel so bad, so sad.
It might sound like a silly thing to say,
but you're a part of me and I'm glad.

You must sometimes wonder about God,
whether the priest really believed in Him.
Did he want to cry out his truth loud!

You must have often needed a friend
to talk to, listen to your frustration and hurt,
must have wondered if it would ever end.

Kid, kid, please don't start to cry.
If there is ever anything I can do,
you can count on me never to lie.

How hard and painful to have known
at such a tender age what lurked inside that man.
Over the years your hurt must have grown.

Look, I was never really all that far away,
always stayed in touch, always listened to you,
and now there is something I want to say:

Kid, kid, to the you I was, I remain true,
loyal to the boy inside the man I became.
I swear: I'll always remember and love you.

Mr. Blues Sings Again

A man is never done singing the gut-bucket blues.
A man ain't ever done singing the gut-bucket blues.
Hear 'em in your head, feel 'em in your toes.

But once you face the blues and start to sing,
yeah, once you feel the blues and start to sing,
you start to whittle away at the monster thing.

Now you ain't goin' to forget forever,
No, you ain't goin' to forget forever,
but you can start to change the weather

that builds up inside your poor head,
storms away inside your poor head
and fills you with a mean old dread.

Sing and soon you don't want to be dead.
Sing your song and you lose some dread.
Sing and you hear something in your head

tells you life ain't always so bad,
go on, stop being always so sad!
You ain't the only one got it bad!

Mama, Tell Me

Mama, oh mama, tell me what to do.
I can tell what the priest wants again
but I can't tell it to daddy or you.

Mama, oh mama, here he comes again.
What can a poor boy like me do?
If he does it to one, he'll do it to ten.

Mama, oh mama, do you feel my shame?
He turns the holy mass I serve for him
into a dirty old man's unholy game.

Mama, oh mama, wherever will this go?
I'm young and want to be full of hope,
but this is bringing me way down low.

Mama, oh mama, sometimes I want to scream.
How could this really be happening to me?
Am I the little boy stuck inside a bad dream?

Mama, oh mama, sometimes I forget my name.
Sometimes when he makes his pushy move
I think there's nobody else but me to blame.

Mama, oh mama, please give me a sign
that you hear me, at least have a clue.
Can't you see I don't know what to do?

Mr. Blues Sings of the Road

Well, I know you couldn't mean me,
Don't mean you're sick and tired of me.
After all, I too am a part of this "we."

We are the man, the boy, and Mr. Blues.
Boy and man make the we, with Mr. Blues.
Good God, what a lot to carry in two shoes!

Come on, let's all go for a walk.
All three of us should go for a walk.
It's way past time we had a good talk.

No car: just a boy, a man, and a blues guitar.
No car: just a boy, a man, and a blues guitar.
Now it's grown dark. Look, see that star?

Every single note I play is one little star.
Every single note I play is one little star.
If enough of 'em shine, we can go far.

We three been walking a good long while.
We three been talking a good long while
as we came down the road mile after mile.

By now we ought to know one another well.
By now we should know one another well,
but how this all shakes down I can't yet tell.

All I know is that when I sing my song,
all I know is that when you sing your song,
the slow process of healing moves along.

What the Boy in the Pastor's Photo Says

You're somewhere under a canopy
of leaves, a boy in a white T-shirt
with some lettering not clearly
visible, but probably having to do
with the Boy Scouts. The priest,
the abuser who instructs you
on how to become a better scout,
not to mention altar boy, lifts his
box camera and squints at you.

The image the pastor makes somehow
survives for over fifty years, bringing
the boy I was back to the man I am.

You have turned, as if asked to,
as if your name had been called.
Your skin is tanned, your hair
cut short in the flat-top of the times,
and your hands are almost folded,
as if in prayer, but fingers stretch
in tension, hands don't come together.

I can hardly bear to look at the pain
in your dark eyes. No boy should
ever have to look this sad and forlorn.
No boy should ever have to reveal
such a depth of darkness in his eyes.
No boy should have to frown, as if
to say, in words he must keep to himself:

What are you going to do to me now?
What do you want and need this time?

Don't you know a picture like this will
tell the whole story to anyone who has
eyes that want to see? When you look
at me through that box camera,
don't you see what the picture will say
about what you were doing to me?
The frown, the lips pressed tight,
the arched eyebrows, the smooth
tender skin of the arms and the face,
the posture of the hands, the play
of the light on the leaves, all say
so much about what you cannot
control in yourself when the urge
comes on that violates all that
you say you are when you try
to act as the priest you vowed
to God you would one day be.

Perhaps this is the only confession
you will ever make, the only
document you will ever sign,
that gives you away for what
you really are beneath the surface.
Is this perhaps the only way
you can admit to what you did?

Boy I was, I want to put my hand
on your shoulder, pull you close,
give you the hug that you need
that does not go where a hug
of a young boy should not go.

I want to adopt you as my son,
tell you it was not your fault,
that you will come through,

that one day you will help
others understand what
it was like to have to keep
such pain in your eyes,
feel it in your delicate hands,
carry it deep in your gut.

I want to be the father who
says, "You can talk to me,
you can tell me what he did,
you can trust me to get it
right when I tell others.
I will not betray you."

When Do the Memories?

Behind any image
that comes out of
an abuser's camera

is another image,
and yet another,
making an album.

When is the album
finished, when do
the memories stop?

Write one poem
and another comes
and another waits

beyond that for
the survivor to
discover it.

No end to
the abuse,
no end to

the succession
of memories
and poems

waiting in line
to push out
into the light.

Hard Times Revisited

As I look back and count the tears
arising from childhood hurt and fears
a sad song lingers in my ears:
hard times, come again no more.

No boy deserves so much sorrow and pain.
No boy should have to stand alone in the rain.
Hard times, hard times, come again no more.
Hard times, stay away from my condo door.

It's a song long and low and sad,
a song that makes me feel so bad.
Hard times, why you have to come back?
Hard times, you torture me on the rack.

It's a song the wind blows down the street,
a song that conjures up a dying lamb's bleat.
Hard times, hard times, come again no more.
Hard times, stay away from my condo door.

Why should a song make a man so weary?
Why should a song make a man so teary?
A long time you been lingering at my door.
Hard times, hard times come again no more.

So many times the song brings back a boy
who just wanted so bad to have back his joy.
Oh hard times, hard times, come back no more.
Hard times, stay away from my condo door.

Hard to Say This

Boy, I know you remember the brother
you loved who played cowboys
and Indians and pitch and catch
and home run derby and smoked
dried corn silk with you in the woods.

Oh my God, how I hate to have to tell
you this, how I wish I could find
words that don't send pain shooting
into your tender heart, but our brother
is gone. Not dead, in the literal sense,
but he up and left over nine years ago,
cut off all ties, became incommunicado,
cannot be reached by the likes of us.
He's alive to some but dead to us:
to me, to our other brother, our little
sister, to his nieces and nephews.

No, no, nothing you did. Something
someone must have done, but when our
brother thinks of betrayal, he thinks of us.
The way our brother feels, the whole
community and place conspired
against him when he was a boy.

Know what, little boy, sweet kid
I remember, it ain't never too late
to talk to those we love. I love you,
I love my older self, I love both
of our brothers and our sister,

I love my wife, I love our children
we adopted from Colombia
and who miss their uncle
who made them laugh so much.

I know this hurts you because
it hurts me too; but now that
we can talk together as the boy
and the man who are one,
we can make it through.
We can pray for our brother
to come back and see that
we never done him wrong.

Mr. Blues Listens Real Hard

Well, I been listening real extra hard,
man, I mean I been listening extra hard
out here in this old barebones yard.

What I can see from way out here,
what I see from this view out here
probably ain't what you see in there.

But my friend, let an old man tell you this,
my good friend, let an old man tell you this:
all God's chil'ren live between pain and bliss.

We all got our heap of sorrow to suffer,
We all got our heap of sorrow to suffer,
But if we learn to talk to one another,

sooner or later good stuff's gonna happen,
sooner or later good stuff's gotta happen.
Brother, this ain't no jivin' empty rappin'.

Let's keep on singing our lowdown blues.
Yeah, keep on singing the lowdown blues
and climb those rungs by ones and twos.

This Is Not the End

Once upon a time there was a priest
who took advantage of young boys,

deceived their parents, and covered
his tracks. But after the boys became

men and could no longer keep quiet,
some of them told the Bishop and

insisted that if he did not speak out
the whole sad story would explode

and many people would be hurt.
The Bishop spoke. Other boys

who were now fathers and grandfathers
gathered the strength to tell their story,

but some still could not take the step.
One day they may be able to make

their move and have their say. You
may even know who they are.

Nobody in any of these stories,
wherever they take place, will

live happily ever after, but if people
can summon what it takes to tell

the truth, they can live together
and help others find their voice.

One voice singing by itself can
sound awfully small, but several

voices lifting as one can make
a chorus that sings a mighty song.

III Tell Me, Pastor

Tell Me, Pastor

Tell me, pastor, tell me, priest,
somebody has asked me
how you changed my life
and I'm not sure what to say.

What could you have done
to make it almost impossible
for me to enter a church
for so many long years?

What could you have done
to make it so painful
for me to say the prayers
you taught altar boys to say?

Tell me, pastor, tell me, priest,
somebody has asked me
how you changed my life
and my words don't work.

What could you have done
to make my little sis wonder
why altar boys have to sleep over
before they serve the early mass?

What could you have done
to so many of my friends
to make them look away when
our parents said your name?

Tell me, pastor, tell me, priest
how you changed my life
because I find it hard to say
what I know I must say.

You were an abomination.
A hot-breath monster.
You defiled us boys
and mucked up our God.

Could you admit that
to my mother and father
who looked up to you
and had you over for dinner?

Could you admit that
to my wife and children
who must wonder why
I grow inexplicably tense?

How else would you explain
when they see me turn livid
because an authority figure
betrays his sacred words?

Tell me, pastor, tell me, priest.
It's your penance more than mine
to tell those who need to hear it
your whole god-damned story.

Questions for a Predator Priest

What did you see
in the mirror each
morning before you
said the mass?

What kind of echo
did you hear when
you prayed to the God
you said you served?

When you put on
the vestments and raised
your hands to bless
our congregation,

what did you see,
what did you think,
what did you feel,
what did you say

to yourself as you
remembered what
you did the night
before to us boys?

How did it feel
to taste in your mouth
the lie you were living
while facing the people?

Was all memory
blocked, all feeling
frozen, all sensitivity
severed at the center?

Sorry

I am sorry
you did what
you did to me
and could not

find it in
yourself to see
or admit that
what you did

violated not only
the boys you abused
and their parents
and brothers and sisters

and their grandparents
and their spouses
and their children
and grandchildren

and the whole community
and the Church
and your fellow priests
and their parishioners

but I will not
surmise what you
said to the God
who had to witness

what you did
when you came
into His presence
and what He

may have said
to force you
to face the evil
you inflicted on us.

Fantasy

I would like to believe
that your eyes and heart
opened before you left

this world of flesh
and spirit and you
admitted to yourself

the wrong you did to others
but it was too late before
you became pure spirit

to turn back and say you
were sorry, you apologize.
Someone must have hurt you

bad to make you hurt us.
I want to believe you left
with remorse, sorrow, regret

and carried your rebirth
with you wherever you went
and are looking back on us

doing your best
as one who saw the light
later than he wishes he had

but still in time to pray
for us even though we
could not know he cared.

But where's a sign?
A hint of proof?
A faint whisper?

Why, Priest, Why?

Why, priest, why
you have to have
so many boys?

Why, priest, why
you have to go
after my friend
and his two
brothers, too?

Why, priest, why
could you never
get enough of boy?

Why you have to
prowl in the pen
night after night
sniffin' for boy

when during the day
you the holy man
of God the Father
singing His song?

What happens to
those manly hands
after they consecrate
the holy Host
and have to go
day after day,
night after night
for boy after boy?

Never enough boy,
never enough touch,
never enough tender
boy meat for you?

Shepherd in the day,
wolf at night,
fang fully exposed,
why, priest, why

you have to deceive
our poor mothers,
fool our fathers,
hoodwink our sisters?

Why you so driven
to go for boy
when you speak
for our God?

Did somebody once
upon a time slam you
up against the barn
and hurt you bad?

Blues for a Priest

Tell me, priest,
did you never
sing the blues?

After you did
what you did
to us boys
and our mothers
and fathers
and little sisters,
did you never
feel low down
dirty and blue?

Tell me true,
priest, after you
did what you did,
didn't you ever
feel like slipping
from Gregorian chant
into the blues?

Priest, sad priest,
I'm so glad I found
the voice to sing
this song for you.

Oh pastor, my priest,
this boy gives you,
as a weekly donation,
twelve bars at a time
the down-home
low-down blues.

Mr. Blues Wakes Up

My friend, I had to go and get some rest.
You know why I had to go get some rest.
Sometimes a little time off works out best.

I'm old and can't follow each and every move.
Old cats can't always follow every single move,
but anybody can see you done found your groove.

Sometimes you sound mad, sometimes I hear glee,
Sometimes you mad, sometimes you got glee.
You keep askin' why this had to happen to me.

Son, I say to you please don't stop singing.
My man, don't ever stop your steady singing,
cause truth and justice be what you bringing.

When you sing it straight, you sure bring it.
When you sing it straight, you really sling it.
Bring the truth and God will pay us a visit.

You and me, we workin' out our salvation.
We doin' all we can to work out our salvation.
One day we sits in the front pew at graduation.

Cautionary Tale in the Pool Room

And there we were down in the bowels
of the school building, in the basement,
in the farthest corner of the empire.

No danger for him, our popular priest.
He was a heavy-handed maniac,
hot for the touch, crazed for boy flesh,

poking with fingers and pressing us
up against the green-felt pool table,
trapping as much boy animal as possible

in his basement lair where he was
safe from the adult parishioners,
including the nuns who taught

us during the day. And what, pray
tell, did he say to us? What sermon
did he give us in the catacombs,

our pastor-man, our parish priest?
What was his cautionary tale?
What once upon a time story did

he share with us, to protect us?
We should be careful how we handle
our tapered pool sticks? Why? Once

upon a time somebody fell on the tip
of his cue and it went all the way up
his anus and reamed out his boy guts.

Go to confession, go to mass every day,
receive communion, and all will be well
in the communion of saints, alleluia.

Bend over boys and put the eight
ball in the side pocket and go back
upstairs and smile in the light, amen.

Statute of Limitations Blues

I got them old statute of limitation blues.
Just can't shake the statute of limitation blues.
I thought it was what you did or did not do,

no matter how much time has elapsed,
no matter how much time has passed,
makes the Church decide if a soul has relapsed.

Somebody tell me, what about right and wrong?
Who will stand strong and talk about right and wrong?
Flip-floppin' ain't no way to write a timeless song!

If a priest does something he should never do,
if a priest does something he should never do,
his salvation depends on when the clock strikes two?

This courtroom morality messes up my head.
This bottom-line business bitches up my brains.
Cheesy theology disturbs the sainted dead.

How hard is it to testify to the truth!
Can't somebody speak the plain old truth?
Or what's gonna happen to our sacred youth?

Holiday Hunt

Did you not realize
when you took a boy
with the men in your family

rabbit hunting on the farm
where you grew up
over the holidays

that one brother would
be a much better hunter
than you and teach

the boy by example
how to do what
a good hunter must do?

That a brother-in-law
with no son of his own
would be a kindly

teacher and explain
to the boy how
to look for signs

in what kind of cover
and where to position
himself when the beagles

were running a rabbit
and keep an eye open
to have a good shot

and show how a boy
hunts best when he knows
he is not being hunted?

Do You Ever Think?

Do you ever think
about the parishioner
who became a priest
because of you?

Do you ever wonder
what he would have
thought or done if
he knew your secret?

Do you know how sad
he became when he
received my letter
telling him the truth?

Do you ever think
how hard it is for him
as an archbishop to deal
with abuse by priests?

A Picture Revisited

When you snapped my picture
which caught the pain
and the sorrow in my
eyes and on my face,

what made you give
it to me to keep?
Did you want my mother
and my father to see it?

Could you not bear to face it?
Could you not rip it to shreds?
Did it make you see
what you were doing to me?

Did you want me to be able
to look at myself fifty years
later and see the boy I was
swallowing such pain?

Did you feel trapped
in the picture of the boy
you caught in your web
and could not let go?

Or did you remain
the predator priest
oblivious to a photo
that does not lie?

A Boy's Yuletide Message to a Priest

Stay away from my Tannenbaum.
Stay away from my crib.
Don't you dare kneel down
and put your filthy hands
on me in my baby bed!

Tables Turned

This time I'm ready.
I look like a little boy
or maybe even a baby.

I've pulled the blanket
up to my chin
and I'm smiling

but my finger
is on the trigger
of a cocked gun.

Step up to my manger,
priest, and I will blow
you to Kingdom Come.

Christmas Card from Mr. Blues

Son, maybe you and the boy should take a break.
Christmas comin' soon, give yourself a little break.
Why not walk with your family around a lake?

I been thinkin' you awful caught up in abuse.
Now what's the use being trapped in abuse?
Times it fires you up, times it drains your juice.

Sometimes I see your spirit sinking low.
Sometimes I feel it sinking down too low.
Go listen to Louie Armstrong's trumpet blow.

Why not listen to your jazz lady friend's piano?
Man, that gal sure can touch and tickle the piano.
Maybe she'll slip you a nice sweet glissando.

My man, look how far you done come in a year.
Lookit what you've gone and written in one year.
Why not sit down, sip and sing some holiday cheer.

Get yourself some winks, catch you some shut-eye.
Yeah, go for the winks, catch you some shut-eye.
Your old friend Mr. Blues, he ain't goin' bye bye!

This old bottlenecker ain't goin' far from you.
He anytime glad to play you somethin' blue.
Ain't no day he ain't a part of what you do.

Double Confession?

Those summers when I was home
from college, how hard I drank.
Worked during the day, played softball
for a tavern or read books at night.
After the games we drank ponies of beer
under the stars; but sometimes on weekends
there was beer in the afternoon and hard
stuff at night. Hard liquor, I mean,
not the young hard stuff you were after.
Hard liquor, binge drinking, big hurt.
Drank so hard I sometimes went blank.

Help me pull it all back. Time to put it
into perspective so my confession
is complete in the eyes of the God
you claimed to represent. I was back
home from college, living in the house
across the street from where you still
kept boys at night so they could serve
the early morning mass for you.

Oh, sure, you know full well what
a hard-drinking town we lived in.
You came from the same culture,
same German Catholic background,
but let's delve deeper. If I'd been aware
of the filth you were doing to so many
other devout Catholic boys who
worked for the parish, I might have
succeeded in drinking myself to death.

But something, maybe a divine act
of mercy, kept me unaware and alive.

I damned near drank myself into oblivion
those summer weekends, sometimes
staggered to work Monday mornings
after stumbling into the house Sunday
night right across the street from
the scene of your pastoral crimes.
I knew I had to get out of town
and go far away to survive,
but could not think about why.
What pain was I driven to make
go dead? What feelings could I not
allow to surface? What childhood
memories could I not talk about
to anyone, not even myself?

Come on, priest, you were the man
with the degrees in theology
and the pedigree in pedophilia.
Admit what you were doing,
trapping one altar boy after another
across the playground and street
where your playboy bedroom
hung in a cloud above the sacristy
in the new Catholic grade school.

If you can't tell yourself,
you sure as hell can't tell me.
I need your help. Fifty years later,
I want to complete my confession.

Back then, I could and would not
admit to you how bad I was hitting
the bottle because I didn't understand
what I was doing and why. Now I do.

My confession will not work, will
not be complete, will not release me,
until you stand up and make yours.
I am prepared to wait a long time.
I'm staring into your eyes, Padre,
and I will not blink or flinch.
My pen is my rifle and my scope
pulls in the blue of your irises.
My aim is good for all eternity.

How You Think My Mama Feel?

How you think
my mama feel
now she knows
what she knows?

Mama felt so good
then knowing
how a man of God
took such interest
in her boys.

She was a mama
loved her man
who had trouble
with his nerves
and tried to
keep him calm.

Mama gave papa
three boys
and one girl
born dead
and one who
stayed alive.

How you think
my mama feel
when it come
to her what
you done to me?

You think her
whole being
not go numb
when it come
to her what
her pastor done?

Priest, you better
go apologize
right now.

You better learn
how to say
a simple s word
end in y
and even that
might not
be good enough.

What you think
my mama feel
who believed in you,
trusted you so much,
came to you for help?

You think she
not feel betrayed?
Slapped and punched
in her farm girl face?

Somebody musta
ripped you apart
and pulled out
and dissected
your heart

to make you do
what you done
to my mama.

How You Think My Daddy Feel?

How you think
my daddy feel
before they
sent him away
to have electricity
shot through
his raw nerves?

You think
he not feel worse
when it come
to him what
you done to me?

Knowing what
you already knew
about how our daddy
looked up to you
and trusted you
and went to you
asking for help

how could you
do what you
did to me?

How could you,
Mr. Priest,
Monsignor Pastor,
Mr. Spiritual Advisor?

You better find
the right words
to say to him
cause he already
felt bad before
you did what
you did to me.

You better find
a way to help
put our daddy
back together
cause you helped
take him apart.

Pedophilia Nursery Rhyme

Burly country priest
gots the hots for boys
and devours their joys
like a famished beast.

His manly appetite
swells at night
and his favorite Venus
is little boy penis.

Catholic Boy Curse

Sir, you are a dirty son of a bitch!
Notice this boy still calls you Sir.
I mean no disrespect to your mother,
but on behalf of my mother and father,
my two brothers and my sister,
and many of my friends, I must say:
Sir, you are a mean son of a bitch.

As you know, we were brought up
to be polite and full of respect,
but I have learned that to recover
from what you did to me,
I must learn how to release
any and all venom still buried
over what you did to so many
of us decades ago for so long.

In honor of fair play and the chance
that you have perhaps changed
since you passed into the world
of spirit, please let me qualify:
Sir, you *were* one son of a bitch!

I Ain't a Kid No More

I ain't a kid no more,
so don't expect me
not to talk back.

Seemed like a long time
you kept me trapped
in my good-boy silence.

Now I'm one mean
son of a bitch!

I howl at the moon.

I been reborn
in the waters
of the word
and I talk back.

I got the sass,
I got the brass,
I got the pen
loaded for bear.

I got all
the ammo I need
and I'm ready
to pull the trigger.

If I were you,
I'd give it up,
come out of hiding
and wave a white hanky.

You can talk.
You can do it.
Just let it rip.

Mr. Blues Listens

You can't give any more than your ear.
The greatest gift is to give all your ear.
Charity is keeping yourself open to hear.

Priest, if I have anything left to say,
if this old man has anything to say,
he say sing in your very own way.

I been singing the blues for many a year,
know what it means to sing year after year.
Priest, I sing but I also give you my ear.

My mama taught me always be kind.
My mama said, you got to be kind.
Seek, listen, and the right song find.

Yeah, you can find the right song to sing.
Listen and you find the right song to sing.
If it ain't your own song, don't mean a thing

IV The Priest on Sorry

Who Are You?

Do not obsess about
what my human hands
may have done

when they were not
consecrating the Host,
baptizing babies,
joining man and woman,
anointing the ill
and the elderly.

Back off, kid.

What my hands
may or may not
have done when
they did not serve
my Maker is between
Him and me.

What I did
to you and others
is on my hands
for all eternity

and will never
wash off

but who are you
to say that
the crippling stain
on my hands

will sink my soul
for all eternity?

What Do You Know?

What do you know
about why I did
what I did to you
and anybody else?

What makes anybody
do what they do
to themselves or
to one another?

What do you know
about why I did
what I did to you
and your friends?

What it was like
to live the difference
between my holy words
and my human hands?

Your hurt is your
story but my
why is a mystery
only God unlocks.

Do You Think?

Do you think
I never felt bad
that my hands

went where they went
and did what they did?
Never felt the pain

of my flesh not
living up to
the sacred vows

I knew I made?
Have you never
violated what you

hold holy? Only then
can you sing my song
of condemnation.

Where Did It Come from?

Where did it come from,
this itch and urge
that made me
always keep boys
in my pound?

How did it hold me
in its grip always
going for one
boy after another,
then his brother?

Did my mother and father
know it was there when
I came into the world?
Or did it come later?

Did my brothers and sisters
see it in my young eyes?
Did they foresee that
cruelty sat at their table?

Did my family always know
a hunger growing in me
would make me crave boys
and lure them into my web
after I was ordained?

If God knew what was
in me before I vowed
to serve only Him,
why didn't He say
No to me when I
said Yes to Him?

If God said Yes to me,
can I be nothing
but evil without
a single trace of good
buried in my soul?

If I Told

If I told boys
never to tell
a single soul
what I did

when I made
them go hard
with the hand that
also held the Host

do you think
I did not know
what I did
was wrong?

If I looked
away when a boy
looked at me
in shocked disbelief

showing hurt
in his eyes,
do you think
I was blind?

Do you think
I never wished
I could stop
the hands

that seemed as if
they belonged to
someone apart
from me?

Don't you ever wish
you could chop off
the hands that take
you into trouble?

Do you never ooze
with a desire so big
and dark you let go
and feel it explode?

Before You Write Me Off

Before you write me off
as a demon monster
with a twisted appetite
don't forget that as a boy
I worked on the farm,
slopped the hogs, fed
chickens, milked cows,
hauled hay, slung manure.

Like you, I fished in creeks
and ponds and rivers, trapped
rabbits in wooden boxes,
hunted squirrels deep in woods,
followed the beagles all day
long in the winter, shucked corn,
mended fences, skinned rabbits
and squirrels and helped butcher.

Hold your tongue, hot-mouth kid.
What gives you the divine right
to condemn me for what I did?
You ain't the only one knows
how to trap a country rabbit.
Take your attitude and shove it.
Write about your own family tree.
To hell with the hard-boiled homily.

Your Mother

Your mother was a good woman,
a good cook and homemaker,
a farm girl who loved to work
inside the house and outside
in the yard and the flower beds
and the vegetable garden.

She knew how to put
all of herself into a prayer
and when I came for dinner
and blessed the food she prepared
it was hard for me to look up
from my plate and make eye
contact with anybody.

It had something to do
with how your mother reminded
me of mine and made me think
of my brothers and sisters
and the father like yours
who was also pretty quiet.

Being in your mother's house
was like being back at home
in the country where I tasted
a darkness swelling from
within into the appetite
that grew dark and wild.

You Wonder?

You wonder what I learned
in the seminary? Well, I knew
I was dedicating myself to
the Highest Cause and lifting
myself up to meet it but all
the while I was with the boys
and young men I felt myself
being pulled or yanked from
down below. Sometimes
I did not know whether up
or down would win the tug
of war and after I got out
following my ordination
and moved into my own
parish I realized the pull
from below could not
be stifled or stopped but still
I looked up to and served
the Higher Cause. The higher
I climbed the lower I sank.
As I continued to sink
lower and lower I spoke
louder and louder on behalf
of what was up on high.

Little Boy Blue Playbill

Why didn't our parents know
you put on such a great show?

They had no clue about the plot.
No idea your hunger was so hot.

While you played your priestly role
stealing our innocence was your goal.

All our parents saw was the pious priest,
no hint of a taste for boys, in the least.

Let's agree on one cold fact:
you sure put on a good act.

When you pulled the curtains shut tight
little boy blue had no chance to fight.

Nuns

Oh for God's sake
how can you ask

if the nuns did not
see below the surface

and wonder what was
going on at night

in my bedroom above
the altar or in my office

during the day. The duty
of a nun is not to ask why

or even dare to wonder if.
The job of a nun is to help

a priest serve God in any
way he knows he must.

Mr. Blues Wakes Up

Somebody got to be puttin' me on.
Ain't no way poor me not bein' put on.
Another voice from beyond and I drown!

The more I listen the less I hear.
The more I listen the less I hear
what rings like truth in my ear.

An old man like me has been around.
A man like me been around and around.
Sometimes words take on a strange sound.

I know why the priest say what he say.
I know why the priest say what he say,
but it make no sense in the light of day.

A man like me knows how hard it can be,
a man like me knows how hard it can be
to find anyone to listen to poor old me.

So I say go and give the priest your ear.
Yeah, go ahead and give him your ear.
If he talks nonsense, kick him in the rear.

Who Needs Dante?

You may talk about
coming clean and getting help
but don't you know that

back then there was no place
to go with the problem
that I had, there was no system

set up to get someone like me
counseling, no tradition in place
in a rural community for a clinic

to operate, no experts to give advice,
no way the Church could admit
to what it had on its weak hands,

no place to send someone like me
except to another parish where
boys were always everywhere

at my beck and call,
no way I could admit
to what I was doing

without bringing total disgrace
on me and my family
and all my parishioners.

What you call my abuse
was perpetuated by the Church
and the parish and the community

and I was promoted to monsignor
and sent to a parish in the country
for the last years of my life

and twenty years later word got out
and they took down my picture
from the back of the church

and took off my name from
the Knights of Columbus chapter
and covered up my name on the base

of the crucifix in the cemetery
and some denied the charges
and some got hurt and angry

and the press came sniffing.
If you want me punished
don't you think it's enough

to see my poor family suffer,
my name sink lower and lower?
Who needs a Dante

to create a vision of Hell
when I made Hell
and left it behind?

Photo Postscript from the Priest

Boy, I am haunted
by that photo I took
of you one summer.
Arms and face tanned

dark, hands open
but also gnarled
in pain, lines
under your eyes.

There is an arch
in your eyebrows
that could come
only from tension.

I cannot remove
myself from
the darkness
in your eyes.

It is as if
I am trapped
inside the image
I made of you.

Your lips are
pressed shut
in the silence
I made you keep.

Thou shalt not
rip this image.
Thou shalt not
throw it away.

Thou shalt stare
into this image
as others stare
into you.

The Boy on His Photo

Now that the whole
wide world can see
what you did to me

I feel so much better.
I give thanks in this letter
to the man I became

for finding the words
to say to the world
what you did to me.

Priest, I give you
this chance to pray
for what you did to me.

I am no longer alone,
sick and sore to the bone.
I pray you may atone.

They say that to forgive
gives one the power to live.
This is your power to give.

Mr. Blues Sings one More

One boy, one man, one priest, and me.
One boy, one man, one priest, and me.
I hope, dear God, we came closer to Thee.

I ain't never gonna stop singin' the blues.
Nope, ain't gonna stop singin' the blues
as long as I got one pair of walkin' shoes.

Men, we done took one mighty long walk.
You bet, together we took a mighty long walk.
Good stuff comes when you learn how to talk.

Now, dear reader, thanks for being such a friend.
Yes sir, yes ma'am, thanks for being a kind friend.
It helped me sing knowin' you had a hand to lend.

Somewhere way down around that big bend,
somewhere way down around that big bend
we're all going to meet again before the end.

Tell you what, though, this whole thing ain't done.
No way, my friend, is this whole big thing done.
We got to go out and have us some good fun.

In my life I seen many a sad and sorry face,
couldn't even tell you how many a sad face.
I say singin' to feel better ain't a disgrace.

When you see in the mirror a face that's long,
when you meet in the mirror a face that's long
it's time to sing yourself a good blues song.

Catfish Boy Blues

Daydreaming on the bank at Grandma's lake
I sat and watched something huge take

my bobber from the surface toward the bottom.
When I yanked my pole I knew I'd got him!

What I pulled in made me cringe and holler:
a deformed catfish wearing a Roman collar!

I took that ungodly fish and gave it a fling.
How could I bear to look at such a thing?

Bad enough to lose almost all your joy
when you're still a defenseless boy.

Maybe it was wrong to pollute the lake
with a freak that had been such a fake.

I wanted to bury deep in the muck
the face that made my religion suck.

The Boy in the Snowy Woods

Snow falls in the night.
In the early morning a boy
leaves tracks trudging
in his boots into the woods.

We have followed the boy
back into that time when
he did not know if he
would ever come back.

Only your silent words
transformed into prayer
that rises above and beyond
any religion can save him.

Let go of your theology.
Step outside of hierarchy.
You must find a new liturgy
and make up a new litany.

To save the soul of the boy
going deep into snowy woods
you must create a new prayer
that rises to God like a hymn.

Alternative Our Father

Our Father who art
above and beyond
yet also within us

speak to the priest
who betrayed this boy
and his entire family

and his parish
and his community
and his church.

Let the priest
find the eyes
to look within

and see and say
what he did wrong
so that the boy

and his family
and parish
and community

can find a way
to forgive but
not forget.

Father, fill
the spirit
of the priest

with understanding
and acknowledgment
of what he did

and let the boy
and his wounded family,
parish, and community

open themselves
to receive the grace
that can heal.

Cut the Crud, Priest

Cut the crud, priest,
why don't you
just come clean?

You taught me
to bait the hook
and pull in the fish,
but it was me
you wanted to hook,
wasn't it, priest?

You taught me
how to hunt squirrels
and let me kill
one you'd wounded,
but it was me you
wanted to shoot down,
wasn't it, priest?

You helped me
become an Eagle Scout,
but it was me you
flew over and preyed on,
wasn't it, priest?

You taught me
how to memorize
the prayers in Latin
so I could serve
your daily and Sunday
mass, but your liturgy
was to seduce a boy,
wasn't it, priest?

You did it to me
and you did it to
too many others,
didn't you, priest?

Cut the crap, priest.
Let it go and for once
just come clean.

Ain't Yours to Say, Boy

Ain't yours to say
when I come clean,
big-mouth boy.

Ain't yours to say
I'm all dirty, boy.

Ain't your place
to ask when
I come clean
or say I got
to talk with God
sooner or later.

How you know
what I feel
when I did
you wrong?

How you know
you the only one
can sing the blues
when you grow up?

Why you think
you got the right
to have Mr. Blues
always on your side?

Ain't a priest who
done wrong to boys
got the right
to sing the blues?

Ain't No Way

Ain't no way
you can tell me
to shut this mouth.

Shoot priest,
you so dumb
you don't know
how long my
mouth had to
be kept shut?

Any kid can
see what's
right and wrong.

Ain't no way
this boy listen
to crap like that.

This mouth
now know
how to talk.

This mouth
got the truth
and the power
of the word
on its side
to speak
loud and clear

for all souls
to hear.

This mouth say
sooner or later you

got to come clean.
This mouth say
time is past when
you can hide.

This mouth learned
when it grew older
how to tell the Bishop
what you done in the dark.

Got him to take down
the picture of you
in the back
of the new church

rip your name off
the banner of
the local Knights
of Columbus Chapter

and jackhammer it
off the base of the big
stone crucifix
in the country cemetery
where your bones lie.

This mouth
knows how to
talk for others.

Priest, you
don't have to
talk to me

but you better
learn how to speak
to your god.

Mr. Blues on Forgive

Guess it's time for this old man to talk.
Clock says time for the old man to talk.
As he said before, this ain't a short walk.

It all comes down to the needs of the boy.
It all comes back to the feelings of the boy.
For him to say he still hurts ain't no ploy.

You people who say hurry up and forgive,
you folks who say press a button and forgive,
forget this poor boy got a whole life to live.

You people who say the boy should rage
up and down across every empty page
are putting him up on your own stage.

The priest who done my boy wrong,
this priest who done me that old wrong
got to find a way to make himself strong.

We all got to step back and wait.
Best if we all step back and wait.
Healing cain't never come too late.

Saint Acid Rain

Robert Johnson said,
Come on in my kitchen,
Goin' to be rainin' outdoors.

He wooed his woman back
with his voice and guitar,
said come into the good place

where I give you what you need.
Priest, you brought a soiled collar
into Mama's kitchen for food.

She invited you in
and you brought along
heavy dark clouds.

When she stood at the stove
she hummed a happy song
and the sun always shone,

but when you came to eat
you brought dark clouds
and the poison rain fell.

I couldn't always see it,
but I sure did feel it.
Did it also fall on you?

How did it strike you?
Like your fingers at night,
your rain stung my skin.

Priest, you came for food
and you brought bitter pain.
You blessed Mama's meal

and then the dark rain fell.
When I hear Robert Johnson's
lonesome guitar wail and ping

like that rain, you come back
into my kitchen wherever
I live. The food tastes good,

but my flesh gets the creeps.
Something I got to say to you.
I call you Saint Acid Rain.

Mr. Blues Counsels the Priest

Even a boy can know the blues.
Even a boy can feel the blues.
Priest, I bring you this news.

What you done to boys is done.
What you done to boys is done
and cain't never ever be undone.

So what you better go and do,
what you gotta make yourself do
is 'fess up so it ain't forever on you.

You go pray hard the Lord have mercy.
Yeah, pray hard the Lord have mercy
so your sins be forgiven by the Almighty.

Not too many words rhyme with mercy.
Ain't many words rhyme with mercy.
Good way to start is an honest *I'm sorry*.

The Boy Sings Along with Brenda Lee

That boy with the blues loved Brenda Lee.
He loved how she sang, oh yeah,
so well, he could feel what she felt.

I'm sorry, little Brenda sang,
with such a big and throbbing voice,
so sorry, so sorry, so sorry.

She was such a big fool, she admitted.
She just didn't know, she confessed,
that love could be so very cruel.

Sometimes when the boy listened to Brenda,
his young ears played a trick on him
and what came out of his mouth

when he sang along with Brenda was,
I was such a fool, such a fool, such a fool
I didn't know a priest could be so cruel.

The Priest on Sorry

Sorry sounds easy to say
until you ask if you
mean it fully forever.

Do you mean you're
sorry you did it because
you should not have

ever done it? Or that
you might get caught
for having done it?

Or do you mean
you're sorry you gave
in to the black urge

that made you brand
your red-hot will
on white lambs?

I don't want to say
the words until they
feel right in my mouth,

until they taste
like a good prayer
I can believe in.

Like an act of contrition
whose every word settles
like stones into the depths.

Like an Our Father
that will lift me
out of this hole.

The Boy Shoves Back

Shove it up your soul!
Shove it up your conscience!
Shove it up your vows!

Shove it up your sermons
and shove it up your breviary.

Shove it up your camping trips
and shove it up your jamborees.

Shove it up your fishing trip
and your hunting in the woods.

Shove it up your Latin prayers
and the water we poured at mass
for you to wash your filthy fingers.

Shove it up your coming over
for dinner to share the food
our mother cooked for us.

Shove it up the spiritual direction
you gave our father when he
was breaking down again.

Shove it up your parish picnic.
Shove it up your shooting match.

Shove it up your parish party
and shove it up your bulletins.

Shove it up your petty policy
of publishing the names of parishioners
and the exact amount each put
in the collection basket for one year
so that everyone could read what
others gave and cluck their tongues.

Shove it up your confession box
where you hid behind the curtain
knowing every voice and the name
of every person who came for help.

Shove it up your ordination
and your jackass jubilee
and promotion to monsignor.

Shove it up your large photo
as the founder of the parish
in the back of the new church
built after you moved away.

Shove it up all you did
to me and my friends
as we grew up looking
to you for guidance

while you pretended
to our parents that you
were the great defender
of all that is right and holy.

Liberation Theology

Priest, get out of my rye field.
Keep your feet off my private path.
You ain't welcome in my tree house.
You ain't invited to my weenie roast.

No, priest, I don't want to go
hunting in your relative's woods.
Guess what, I done found
my own squirrel hunting woods.

Priest, keep your hands off
each and every solitary one
of my rabbit traps, unless
you want to get caught!

No, no way I want to go
fishing in your lake or pond.
Don't matter to me if the lake
is next to your family farm.

I got my own fishing holes.
I got my own good river.
I got my own family lake.
My own rod and reel and bait.

Priest, your day is done.
I'm my own little man.
I got my own will, my own
place, and my own voice.

This Is Your Life

The cameras are focused on you.
You're in the chair on stage
and here come the relatives,

your parents, aunts and uncles
your brothers and sisters,
and a few of the cousins.

We'll find out what you were
like when you were a little boy,
what you said and did and liked.

Don't worry, the relatives still love you
and want only to help tell your story.
They are grateful for a chance to talk.

The stories they tell will help us
understand why you acted as you did.
Somebody must have hurt you bad.

Now your father talks about your
grade-school graduation speech.
Your parish priest tells a little tale.

You are graduating from seminary.
You are ordained, become pastor
of a new parish. And now it's over.

Singing in the Slammer

Priest, priest, does a boy
have to tell a man like you
what they do to sex offenders
behind bars when the lights
go off? Don't turn your back.
Don't dare fall asleep.
There's an angry vigilante
in every nook and cranny.

You got to sing, priest,
sing for your eternal soul,
sing for your salvation,
sing and say you're sorry.
Say I didn't know what
I was doing. Say I couldn't
control the darkness rising
up and flooding over me.

Pedophile Priest Confession

Look, I know what I did.
I know what The Book says
I should not have done.

If I ever had it all over again,
I don't know if I could
stop myself from groping

young boys. What's deepest
inside a being doesn't
convert to the other side

overnight. Or over
the duration of one
man's lifetime. No falling

off the horse on this one.
No burning bush to exorcise
the ache for fresh boy flesh.

No voice telling me to sacrifice
my own son, but I held a blade
to many a boy's throat.

No thunder on the mountain,
no lightning across the sky
ever signaled His opposition.

So I never stopped.
Damn it, I am what I am.
Ain't no pill invented

by the biggest brains alive
to stop me from craving
what I lived to have: boy.

Ain't no prayer been written
for pedophile priests. Ain't
no Patron Saint of Pedophiles.

Maybe I still don't want
to stop. Maybe I can
never get enough

of what I know I should
not have. Maybe getting
caught would be the worst

sin I could commit. If you
want to pray for me anyhow.
go ahead and be my guest.

Instead of Mr. Blues, maybe
Saint Jude, patron saint
of hopeless cases, is my man.

Home Burial

I'll wait until after dark,
so nobody can watch.

I know your bones have settled
in the ground for twenty years.

It's the memory of what you did,
not your body or soul, I must bury.

Don't worry, we no longer own
the brick house, but these feet

know the way back in the dark.
I promise not to disturb a soul.

I've already dug a black hole
in which I will lay your memory.

I'll settle the good Midwestern earth
over you like a warm cozy blanket.

I may even fold it back and tuck
you in so you sleep for the duration.

Don't forget, I know the sound
of your voice. I am always

on call if you can find a way
to say exactly the right words.

Priest, you know what they are.
We both believe in their power.

So here I now leave you in a bower.
I leave you to reflect, hour after hour.

Mr. Blues on Home Burials

Well, I'm glad you put him away.
I like the way you put him away.
Anybody can see it's now your day.

Maybe somebody's dog gonna bark.
Red rooster will crow, hound dog bark
when he smells old memories in the dark.

Dirty old memories don't up and die.
Painful memories don't suddenly die.
Storm clouds don't open to clear blue sky

without a heavy rain fallin' down,
without a hard rain dumpin' down.
I'm bettin' you gonna leave this town.

Boy, I say again I'm right proud of you.
This old man be forever proud of you
for doin' what you knew you had to do.

You stared into the eye of the beast.
You went back and fought that beast.
You would not give in to that priest.

I like the way you gave him a chance.
You got a big heart to give him a chance.
If he say he sorry, you can do your dance.

My boy, I got to give it to you.
This old man hands it to you.
To your young self you been true.

Love Song for Mr. Blues

Long time you been my good friend.
Long time you been my pal and friend.
In my long silence, you helped me mend.

You spoke to me about the presence of pain.
So well you translated the language of pain,
in times of sunshine, cloud, and hard rain.

Always, always you spoke right to me.
Never a time you didn't talk to me.
You showed me how to break free.

Always in my ear I heard your voice.
Your guitar spoke like a human voice.
You made me believe I had a choice.

Sometimes you sang like Robert Johnson.
Sometimes you were Blind Lemon Jefferson.
Sometimes Lightnin' Hopkins, Charlie Patton.

You taught a young man how to cope.
Yes, you showed me I could cope,
laugh, and bounce back off the rope.

Your blues dove deep inside of me,
became one with the spirit in me
and taught me what it means to see

there's always a hopeful boy inside the man.
Deep down lives a hopeful boy inside the man
won't quit fighting till he comes out best he can.

Epilog: Words of a Good Priest
for Fr. Michael O'Mara

I dreamed I would meet a priest
who would not do me wrong
as one did when I was a boy.

He would understand the hurt
I felt as a boy carried by
the man and father I became.

This priest would say I'm sorry
as the other one never could do.
This priest would live the words he said

just as the son of a carpenter once did.
As I would hear this priest speak
from the pulpit, he would open

a line between the life he lived
deep within himself
and the life we as a community

were building for ourselves.
Some call this the life of the spirit,
crossing from one soul to another.

This priest would open channels
between himself and us
and we would recognize his words

as coming from beyond himself
and sometimes burn like coals
as they passed into him

but soothe and heal as they entered
into us, challenging us to grow.
Sometimes these words he gave us

would make us understand
more clearly what we already
sensed but could not say.

Sometimes his words gave us strength.
Sometimes they entered so deeply
into us that the only way we could

say them was as a prayer
that arose as if from within us
and became an utterance we did

not recognize as ours but
knew it was what he would
leave with us to say together

when it came time for him
to move on to another life
he would build within others.

What he left us was lived words
of the spirit to keep us alive, just
as we gave him love to carry on.

There will be water running
from a fountain in a grotto
and roses blooming anew.

There will be lasting memories
of growing together with him in spirit
as his words continue to open in us.

Acknowledgments

Some of these poems originally appeared in *Branches* ("Alternative Our Father," "Prayer for Survivors," "The Way into the Woods"); *Cybersoleil* ("Mr. Blues and Etheridge Knight"); *From the Edge of the Prairie* ("Not Even Isaiah and Jeremiah," "To Some Blues Mamas and Papas," "To Hildegard of Bingen," "To Mechthild of Magdeburg," "To Dorothy Day"); *Relief: A Christian Literary Expression* ("My Father's Wake"); *Pilgrimage* ("To Isaiah"); and *The Tipton Poetry Journal* ("This Is Not the End"). "Angel of Power and Protection" was written as part of an Airpoets (Joyce Brinkman, Ruthelen Burns, Joseph Heithaus, and Norbert Krapf) project to create poems inspired by the photography of Denis Kelly to be included in an exhibit of his Sacred Places series at the Indiana Interchurch Center of Indianapolis and was also part of the anthology *Airmail from the Airpoets* (San Francisco Bay Press, 2011). "Words of a Good Priest" was written at the request of Rev. Michael E. O'Mara to celebrate his 25th anniversary as a priest and read by the author at the 15 June 2013 mass at St. Mary's Parish, Indianapolis to commemorate that occasion. Thanks to the editors of these publications for their earlier support.

The author wishes to thank Sr. Wanda Wetli, CSJ, Patricia Ley, and Jan Gildner for their expert guidance and support; John Groppe for his literary assistance and steadfast encouragement; William Heyen for the sharp knife that helped the author prune for shade; Fr. Michael O'Mara for his uplifting compassion; Chuck and Barb Stevenson and Greg and Kriss Ziesemer for their loving friendship; Katherine, Elizabeth, and Daniel Krapf for listening, waiting, and not flinching too often; Matthew Fox, whose work and friendship, arriving after the poems were drafted

but not yet in final book form, gave a large boost of
support, encouragement, and the confidence to persist;
Jason Berry, Andrew Harvey, and Michael D'Antonio
for their affirmations; Mari Evans for speaking from her
whole heart; Phil Gulley, for his Hoosier sense of humor,
straight-talking Quaker theology, and powerful book *If the
Church Were Christian*; and Elsa Kramer and Tom Healy of
Branches for the hospitality.

Thanks to Franconian friends Helmut Haberkamm and
Petra Däumler for open ears and patient suggestions;
J.G. for the camaraderie; Rebecca Luzio, former Victim
Assistance Coordinator of the Diocese of Evansville, for
her sympathy and appreciation; former Bishop Gerald
Gettelfinger for approving immediate assistance and
making an important and timely public announcement;
and Judy Neff for her steady vigilance. Thanks to my
sister Mary and the many friends, including my successor
as Indiana Poet Laureate and pew mate, Karen Kovacik,
Jeanetta Calhoun Mish, Sharon Gamble, Julie Roe
Lach and Cathleen and Eduardo Krebs for listening and
encouraging me to begin writing and persist. Later thanks
to documentary filmmaker Susanne Schwibs for the eye,
ear, and voice to say yes to this story that had to be told
in more ways than one. Thanks also to Richard Beck for
understanding it all and to Gordon Bonham for helping
me find the shuffle in E to play behind the title poem and
opening my ears to music for other poems. Finally, to my
old Delta friend over the decades, Mr. Blues, thanks for
staying with me so long and helping me heal in the kitchen.

About the Author

Norbert Krapf, Indiana Poet Laureate 2008-10, was born in Jasper, Indiana in 1943. In 1965, he received his B.A.in English from St. Joseph's College (Indiana), which thirty years later gave him an honorary doctorate. He received his M.A. and Ph.D. in English from the University of Notre Dame in 1966 and 1970, with a concentration in American Poetry, and is emeritus professor of English at Long Island University, where he taught for 34 years and directed the C.W. Post Poetry Center. He served as U.S. Exchange Teacher at West Oxon Technical College (1973-4) and as Senior Fulbright Professor of American Poetry at the Universities of Freiburg (1980-81) and Erlangen-Nuremberg (1988-89). He received the Lucille Medwick Memorial Award from the Poetry Society of America (1999) and had a poem included in a stained-glass panel by English artist Martin Donlin at the Indianapolis International Airport (2008). Garrison Keillor has read his poems on The Writer's Almanac. Since 2004, Krapf has lived with his family in downtown, Indianapolis.

Krapf's ten full-length poetry collections often explore his German-Catholic heritage, such as *American Dreams: Reveries and Revisitations* (2013); *Songs in Sepia and Black and White* (2012, photos by Richard Fields); *Bloodroot: Indiana Poems*, a selection from poems collected 1971-2006 and also new work (2008, photos by David Pierini); *Sweet Sister Moon*, celebrations of women (2009); and *Blue-Eyed Grass: Poems of Germany* (1997), which concludes with a cycle about WW II and the Holocaust. He is the editor of *Finding the Grain: Pioneer German Journals and Letters from Dubois County, Indiana*

(2006), which includes the letters of missionary-colonizer Joseph Kundek, and also the editor-translator of *Beneath the Cherry Sapling: Legends from Franconia* (1988) and *Shadows on the Sundial: Selected Early Poems of Rainer Maria Rilke* (1990). He is the author of a prose memoir, *The Ripest Moments: A Southern Indiana Childhood* (2008). For *Catholic Boy Blues*, he received an Alpha and Omega Arts Award for religious risk presented during the Indianapolis Spirit and Place Festival 2013.

As Indiana Poet Laureate, Krapf promoted collaborations and the reunion of poetry and song. He has released a CD with German-born jazz pianist and composer Monika Herzig, *Imagine: Indiana in Music and Words* (2007), and he also collaborates with bluesman Gordon Bonham. Krapf and Bonham began performing together as part of the Hoosier Dylan show. Krapf received a Creative Renewal Fellowship 2011-12 from the Arts Council of Indianapolis to continue to reunite poetry and song, with an emphasis on the blues. His fellowship activities included several trips to Memphis, the Mississippi Blues Trail, and blues festivals. He has served on the board of Etheridge Knight, Inc. For further information and audio and video files of performances and readings, as well as an Indiana Poet Laureate Photo Gallery, visit www.krapfpoetry.com.